HAPPY DAY
HEARTBREA

A farmer's son relives hi

HAPPY DAYS AND HEARTBREAK DAYS

A farmer's son relives his 1920s childhood

Victor William Dilworth

Dedication:
To Olive, my late wife,
For fifty-two years of love, happiness and three wonderful sons.
"Thank you".
VWD

ISBN
1 901253 34 1
First published November 2003

Published by:
Léonie Press
an imprint of
Anne Loader Publications
13 Vale Road, Hartford,
Northwich, Cheshire CW8 1PL Gt Britain
Tel: 01606 75660   Fax: 01606 77609
e-mail: anne@leoniepress.com
Website: www.anneloaderpublications.co.uk
www.leoniepress.com

Printed by:
Anne Loader Publications
Collated and bound by: B & S Swindells Ltd, Knutsford
Covers laminated by: The Finishing Touch, St Helens

About the author

I'm now in my eighties but still young at heart. This book is about my memories as a small boy who was born into a Shropshire farming family. My father had been married before he met my mother so I had two stepbrothers, Charles and Bert. Their mother had died at the time of Bert's birth. When our father married my mother they started a second family: my sister Muriel was first, followed by Harold, then Cyril and me six years later. I always say I am the scratching of the pot.

There was always a good warm feather bed and wholesome food – boiled potatoes and carrots, roast or boiled beef followed by farmhouse rice pudding, not forgetting home-made apple pies and the like. What we all enjoyed were Mother's fruit cake and crusty pork pies. Most of the food we had was produced on the farm.

When I finished my schooling I went to work as an agricultural engineer; perhaps I was tired of farming. As the farm was only a hundred acres, my father said it would be better if I went and got my own living, for there were plenty of hands at home.

So why not share my days of happiness and heartbreak with me?

Victor William Dilworth

Victor Dilworth pictured as a schoolboy,
proudly wearing the lapel badge of the
Daily Mail's "Teddy Tail" children's club

Contents

This is the story – described through a child's mind
and eyes – of my experiences being brought up within a
farming family in the Twenties, with strict parents of
Victorian moral standards, when work and obedience
were of great importance.

I hope it is written in a way to provoke thought
and give enjoyment.

V W Dilworth
October 2003

INTRODUCTION

Rebirth

Making a return journey from Wales to my home in the East Midlands, I took a route which passed through the Shropshire village where I was born and attended my first school. The day itself was nothing particular. The only thing was the rain which at times was running down the car windscreen. The skies were overcast and the sun occasionally peeped through the clouds. It was not a day to see the best of the country.

The conversation with Olive, my wife, was about everyday topics, like our children who have now grown up and fled the nest to make their own way in the world. Time and miles passed by when all of a sudden I realised I was in the village of so many memories. It is not like one thinks a village should be – with houses, a church, a school and a public house built in a kind of a close circle. It has a shop, a public house, a few scattered cottages, a war memorial and, three quarters of a mile down the main road, the church. This is surrounded by a few more cottages, the village hall and another public house. It gives the impression that some lord of the manor once walked along this two-mile stretch of the highway with a large shovel of cement and as bits fell off he would say, "Build here, or there," until the shovel was empty, and the largest lump was the church.

I slowed down passing the school, giving me time to point it out to my wife – remarking that it was a few years since I

1

had played in that schoolyard. Then we drove on, recalling things that I remembered as a child in the area.

Then silence took over, as it does on a long journey. I watched the road, the wipers going backwards and forwards across the windscreen, thinking more about my childhood. I thought of my parents, long since passed away, lying in the churchyard which we had not long left behind, and my sister and brothers. How we lived on the farm together and the things we did – happy days and heartbreak days. By the time I was coming to my journey's end the feeling was strong within me that I wanted to return to the farm, home of my birth.

I promised myself I would do this some day. There was no opportunity at that time, for my mind was concentrated on the material things in life, earning money, providing a home for the future and not dreaming of days long gone, never to return. I wondered, if it were possible to relive those days, would they be true to what I thought they were? As my mother would say to us, "You can't put a fallen apple back on the tree." This saying puzzled me as a child, for I thought I could tie the apple on the branch again with a piece of string. But years passed and I began to understand what she meant.

One arrives at that milestone in life when the modern word 'retirement' is mentioned, or as the old countryman would say, "tak ye old horse out of the harness and let him peacefully graze in the meadow."

Yes, my wife and I have arrived at the meadow blessed, we think, with good health and very few visible scars of our journey through life, but with an abundance of love between us and some of that caring and understanding we had given to the children being returned, in each of their particular ways. The bright eyes of the grandchildren, and the warmth reflected through them, is something only the grandmas and grandpas among us can appreciate. It makes one feel like having a gallop around the meadow, but like the old horse, the flesh and bones soon tire.

The days of work shortened, giving us more time to think and do things together that we'd always wished to do. The memories of the past flooded back into the mind. I enjoyed the evenings by a good log fire listening to the click of knitting needles as my wife was busy making something for someone's birthday.

As for me, I was content to sit, watching the flames of the fire dance about and vanish up the chimney forever, only to doze off in the warmth of the armchair and dream of childhood days. I felt a compelling urge to retrace my steps through a period of my life in which every day brought new experiences and wonderment. Yes, I dreamt on, shutting out even life as it is now. Beginning that journey conjured up the memories, but they were not just memories, if you understand, more a real truth.

Suddenly I am asking questions, seeing, touching; walking into a vacuum created by the passage of what we call time.

The journey feels like reality, as my imaginary car rushes along roads, passing through villages as if there is no other traveller on this earth. I am alone. Soon I find myself driving in the village of my birthplace; travelling through the lane, not as they know it today, tarmac and smooth, but bumpy with stones, the gravel being tossed about as the wheels bounce over the surface. Trees with their new leaves of spring are bowing and tossing, as if to welcome me back. Birds sing, flowers in the hedgerows are in abundance. Flowers which I'd not seen since childhood – harebells, buttercups, primroses and small wild violets pushing up between their taller neighbours, saying "Let me be seen, for I am pretty too". I feel I am taking a flower from here and there but I never hold them in my hand.

The car vanishes from my journey and I find myself walking down a lane which I know. As the sun shines I can feel a warmth of welcome. Then, as things become vivid, a chilled feeling envelops me, so ghostly, yet like some mysterious hand outstretched to call me forward. I walk down the lane noticing the gate with a broken rail and a nearby holly bush, its boughs crowding over the path. I walk on around the bend past the tall ash tree, and arrive at the gate which opens into the farmyard. Things become more clear as I dream on. Turning across towards the house I can see the section of stone wall which I rebuilt and the footholds into which we children put our feet to give us a lift as we jumped over it.

I soon come to the back door of the house through which I enter, yet I cannot recall opening it. For at that moment everything becomes dark, mysterious, as if I have lost my way. Soon I begin to experience the light and the feeling of warmth again. At the same time, things wrapped around me restrict my movements. I pull at what is making me restless but the light fades and comes back again. Then, for no reason as far as I can tell, the images of my mother and father become living persons to me. Time adds on my sister and brothers until they are real people towering above me, at times frightening. I begin to respond and react to the sound of their voices until I feel as one with them, realising I am part of the family to which a bond is formed, recalling what I did as a child, crying, playing and sharing my life with one and all. It has all become so real.

CHAPTER ONE

Early Childhood

Now I am aware that I am a member of a family, recognising father, mother, brothers and sister; sounds of talking, laughter and voices raised in anger.

I can recall the kitchen where we used to sit, talk, work and eat. Along one side was a bench seat scrubbed white with an equally white table. Father always sat at the end of this bench near to the fire and I sat next to him. For some reason I felt frightened of him, for to me he was a big man, with a white hairy moustache which wobbled about as he ate. There was silence from the others seated around the table. A cushion was provided for me to sit on because I couldn't reach my plate. Soon I would fidget and tire of sitting, then after I'd been moving about for a short time, the cushion would slip from under me. Father would stop eating and, with fork and knife in mid-air, turn in temper and exhort, "For God in Heaven, will you sit still?" accompanied by a hard push with his elbow. A tear would roll down my cheek in fear. After bowing my head I would look over to my sister Muriel, for by this time I had found out that this was from where my comfort would come on such an occasion.

After I'd moved about trying to retrieve my cushion, Father would start to rise in anger and before words could come out of his mouth, Mother, who sat at the end of the table with her back to the fire, would jump up, reach over and grip hard on my arms to lift me from my seat. Then she'd bump me hard down on my bottom onto an old stool in the corner well away from the table. There I'd sit, silently sobbing, for I knew if I made a noise black looks would be coming my way. When the meal was over and all but my sister had left the kitchen, she would come over to me with warmth in her voice and hands outstretched, lifting me up, wiping my tears away and saying, "Come on, let's go out and see Rover." As we went through the door into the yard, she would hug me tight to her, giving me that important kiss. As we stood in the yard talking and patting the dog my mother's raised voice would be heard to say, "Put that child down and get on with some work." Without hesitation Muriel would leave me, sometimes sitting with Rover sharing the old sacking on which he had made his bed, or she would divert my attention towards the odd toy which was lying about.

As the months went by I began to explore, excited by what was happening around me. Soon thoughts and words became important; more and more, they were to have a meaning in my relationship with others. I would relate to the feelings and material things around me. Even the farmyard, which before was just somewhere for me and the dog, became a place to explore. I can remember the gates at the bottom of the yard through which I would peep to watch the cows coming in to be milked and the horses drinking at the water trough. It was a barrier through which I was not allowed to pass.

On the other side of the yard were a coal shed and pigsties. Being too small to see over the door of the sty I used to give it a kick, then look through a crack to see the pigs jump up and rush to the door, thinking food was on its way. Although I did it time and again it frightened me when the pigs pushed on the door. Sometimes I would pull up grass and throw over it to hear them snuffling and fighting for what I had thrown in. Soon I would tire of this and return into the house. This was the time when I really began to understand what people were, not just figures bigger than me. Names were important.

Muriel meant more than just being my sister. My brothers Harold, Bert and Cyril were people along with my mother and father. It was part of sharing the same food, sitting by a fire in the same room, laughing and talking, learning about reactions, asking questions, understanding 'No' and 'Yes' by the tone of voice in which they were delivered; holding conversations, being told the difference between right and wrong, work and play.

Everything excited me: the smell around the house and in the yard outside, the songs of birds in the hedges. Soon I was asking "What's this or that?" only to be told "You want to know too much at your age. Shut up and be quiet!"

This worried me and I would go away sulking, asking myself why grown-ups were so awful. I was often still thinking about this when I went upstairs to bed, wishing I were grown-up too.

In the mornings I would awake to the sounds of people scurrying about, their steel-tipped clogs ringing out as they came into contact with the quarry tile floors, and the noise of buckets being emptied – their handles rattling when they were put down on the floor. This made me wonder what was going on downstairs. Soon I was awake enough to raise myself out of my warm feather bed to wander down the stairs in bare feet, which came into contact with the cold, cold tiles as I stepped into the kitchen. Clad only in my nightshirt I would make for the only mat by the kitchen range. After warming my body as the fire burnt brightly I would look around the door leading into the dairy, only to find Harold carrying pails of milk from the cowsheds. Seing me standing there he'd remark, "Mind the ducks don't come and get your little willy!" Immediately, I would push my shirt down between my legs and rush back to the fire.

Mother, at this time in the middle of preparing breakfast, would take my clothes down from the rack hanging from the ceiling to dress me. Sitting on my stool, I could observe the range. On one side of the fire was a boiler, which they would fill with water. On the front of the boiler was a shiny brass tap from which they would draw off the boiling water; on the other side of the fire was the oven, with a flat top on which would be a saucepan of oat porridge steaming away. In the oven the home-cured bacon would be cooking. How I recall the smell of that cooking bacon! Hanging over the fire was a steaming kettle ready for making coffee. Mother would bring slices of home-made bread and a long toasting fork for me to toast the bread for breakfast.

Soon my brothers would begin coming in for breakfast, picking up a dish and helping themselves to porridge from the saucepan. Then they'd take their places around the table, where the conversation would be about how many gallons of milk had gone into to the vat for the cheese-making and which cow had calved in the night. After all this, Father would detail the work required to be done for the day. My brother Cyril would prepare and leave for school while my brother Bert went out to feed the pigs. As soon as they heard buckets being filled with their food from the bins they would push on the doors of their pens, squealing loudly. As Bert opened the door they would rush out, only to return as quickly when the food was tipped into the trough. When the buckets were empty he would give me one to carry back for a refill. I loved helping him, for it made me feel grown-up. Feeding over, Bert would go into the cowsheds to carry out other tasks.

I would play with one of the dogs – for by this time I had collected odd boxes, old pram wheels, string and chain. A box would become a cart with pieces of string and I would harness the dog to the 'cart' to become the 'horse'. Sometimes he would do as I wanted, other times he sat down refusing to budge. Father would come by, and on seeing the dog tangled up in the string harness, he'd put his hand in his pocket, take out a pocket knife and bend down, cutting the dog free. Then he'd turn to me to tell me not to do it again. But he never explained why, for it seemed to me then that he had not the time to talk. This incident all over and done with, I would wander in the dairy to watch what was going on. Steam would be rising from a big boiler. Muriel would be bending over the milk vat. I see now her arms pushing down into the milk. All this was one big mystery to me. As she raised her arms from the milk she would take me out of the dairy explaining that the boiling water could hurt me. Although I did not want to leave, she would always have time to find something else to occupy me.

The days went by. I began to take a more active part in what was going on around me. People's attitudes towards me were changing. I was allowed to go through that yard gate, which up to now had always been a barrier to me, coming more in contact with other farm animals, horses, cows, calves and hens – and chicks, as they rushed around with the mother hen. I now felt grown-up, a 'big boy' if you like. This realism was becoming a more important part in my play. As Harold and Cyril had done before me, I would collect sticks of different lengths and thickness. I would arrange stones in the shape of the farm buildings, then place the sticks in position. These would become my cows and the smaller sticks represented calves. To get a difference in colour, like the real cows, I would take some of the bark from the stick to reveal white patches of the wood. For horses, the sticks were much longer; pigs were always represented by empty tin cans of all shapes.

This make-believe world would be all arranged and played out behind the stone wall in the orchard. Oh, the happiness these pieces of stick gave to me, for I would act out the things I was experiencing in the grown-ups' world.

My father seemed to take more interest in me now, for he started to take me with him around the farm. Some mornings he would be going to feed sheep in a far-off field. Firstly, he had to load hay and corn into the float to which he would harness the pony. As the pony was sometimes restless while the preparations were going on I was told to hold her head to stop her wandering off.

One momentous day, with everything needed on board, Father lifted me high on the hay in the float. Then he jumped up, sitting on the hay and corn, and with the reins in hand we set off. As we left the farmyard, Mother was standing by the gate. I gave her a wave of my hand as we went past. This was a big moment for me. For the first time I was doing something worthwhile with my father. All of a sudden, he did not seem so powerful, for I felt as big as him.

As we left the yard, Father gave a quick flick on the reins and a "Come on, Dolly." Dolly was not a pony like those used for riding, but what is known as a 'cob'; with her shorter body – more rounded than a riding pony's – and her thicker legs, she was more suited for pulling light loads just as we had that morning. Dolly started trotting up the lane a little faster. The iron-rimmed wheels bounced and clicked over the gravel surface. The float swayed from side to side and the chill of the wind blew into my face. This did not seem to matter for I was glowing warm inside with excitement: my first ride to the sheep with my father! Dolly trotted on as if she knew where she had to go, for when I glanced over to Father I saw he was not concentrating on driving her but was studying the fields beside the road. While I was looking he turned, put his hand on my head, ruffled my woolly hat and with a warmth in his voice I had never experienced before said, "How do you like this, my son?" He made me feel wanted on the journey: I cannot tell you how I felt inside. I began to watch the pony and the harness which held her in the shafts. The reins lay loosely on her back, the long brown hair of her tail brushed against the front of the float. By now the heat of her body could be felt on my face; I could smell the warm leather harness and the hay on which I was sitting. All this was so new and exciting.

I could only think about what my father had said a little earlier and wish the journey could go on forever. I felt that Father was mine alone. Then, with a light tug on the reins and a "Woo," Dolly turned into the gateway of the field. With a smile Father gave me the reins to hold while he got down off the float. As he opened the gate I held the reins and then he led Dolly into the field. As the gate closed behind us he came back on the float and quietly took back the reins.

Soon the sheep heard my father calling. They began to come from everywhere: lots of them, some running, some walking and some bleating, others running too fast, unable to make a sound. Father got down off the float. He seemed to stand looking at each and every one as if he knew them individually by name. They milled around the float, their faces – some black, others white – all looking up at me and the feed we had brought.

Father started to take off the bags of corn, walking over and emptying the contents from the sacks into a long line of troughs. The sheep jumped and jostled for position. Then hay was taken from the float and placed into the hayrack nearby. With all the food emptied out, Father returned. Dolly began walking quietly from the field. As we came onto the road Father closed the gate and looked back at the sheep as if he didn't want to leave them. He jumped into the empty float and with another quick tug on the reins Dolly trotted back down the lane towards home.

In the fields we saw rabbits running about. In one of the fields Massey the waggoner was ploughing, the pair of big Shire horses walking a steady pace. As they approached the roadside, their heads nodding to and fro, Massey could be heard talking to them. Soon they were at the end of the furrow. As they turned, Father exchanged a few words with Massey. Then we continued down the lane back home. As we stopped in the yard Father lifted me down. As soon as my feet touched the ground I could not run fast enough to the house. As I went in the first person I met was Mary, one of the maids. When she enquired where I had been I could not get the words out fast enough for excitement. During the time I was telling her everything she had made me a cup of cocoa, which I soon drank. Then I went out to my farm of stick animals behind the orchard wall, reliving every moment of my morning's experience. Soon I heard Muriel calling me in for my dinner. As she helped me wash my hands I had to tell her all I had seen that morning. In fact as we all sat at the table it was the main topic of conversation. Everyone in the room listened to my story. Soon everyone left the kitchen. Dishes were removed from the table for washing up in the scullery. This is where all the household work was carried out, including cheese and butter making. It was not a place for me at this time in the day, when they were busy scrubbing the floors and the equipment that had been used during the morning's cheese-making.

In the early afternoons, my sister Muriel and brother Bert would be packing the new cheese curds into the cheese tubs. These tubs were made from wood bound with iron bands around the sides and had holes in the bottom through which whey would drain as the cheese press was screwed down, compounding the curds until it looked like the solid cheese that you see in the shops. To allow this compounding the tubs were lined with cheesecloth and curds taken from the curd mill were emptied into the tubs until they were full. Then a loose metal sleeve that extended the height of the tub was placed into the top and more curd was added. At all times they pressed down on the curds with their hands. Then the cloth was folded over the curds. The full tubs would be placed into the presses that stood to one side of the scullery. A press was a kind of metal frame with a base on which the full cheese tub was placed. When this was done a board was placed over the tub. Then my sister would wind down a metal plate connected to a long threaded rod attached to the top of the press frame. As the press came down it pressed onto the metal band. As pressure came down on the tub the curds were pressed down into it. As the curds became more solid the remaining whey would begin to run out of the holes around the tub and was collected in buckets placed underneath the press. Pressing took some time, as the press was screwed down at intervals until all whey stopped dripping from the tub.

While all this was going on my brother Bert filled the big boiler – which had already boiled water in the morning for the cheese-making – with potatoes for the pigs. To this day I can recall the smell of these steaming hot potatoes in their jackets. This was an exciting time for me. I would stand by the boiler watching potatoes cook. Mother would come from the kitchen from time to time and say, "Keep away, you'll get scalded." She would push me outside to go and play. Rover would be sitting outside the back door for he knew that it would soon be pig-feeding time and he might get some tit-bits of food.

Some of the steaming hot potatoes would be taken out of the boiler, put into a big bin and mixed with the pig food. As this was being done, my brother would select a whole potato and after cooling it, would give it to me to eat. In winter I would more likely have put it in my pocket to warm my hand.

Soon my brother Cyril would come home from school. The first thing he would do would be to go into our long pantry, only to return with a big piece of fruit cake or a slice of cold apple pie. This eaten, he would change into working clothes, for he was five years older than me and this meant that he had jobs to do around the farm including getting in the next morning's sticks and coal which would be neatly placed by the boiler in the scullery. Sometimes, I would go and help him but he would always leave me a bucket full of coal too heavy for me to carry. Then he would return and on seeing my plight would tease me saying that I had sparrow's knees. This would hurt me and make me cry. I would wander back into the house to sit by the kitchen fire sucking my thumb, feeling unwanted and rejected. Mother often at these times was preparing the evening meal. She'd look down at me, saying, "Stop sniffling boy – go and get your hands washed and get from under my feet." At this time of the day I hadn't my sister to go to for comfort, for she was taking part in the milking.

Often at such times I would watch through the kitchen window to see the buckets of milk being carried up the yard into the scullery to be emptied into the large milk vat ready for the next day's cheese-making. From the window I could see Bert preparing the pigs' food from the bin in the yard. As he carried the buckets toward the pigsties I could hear the pigs jumping at the doors, squealing. The food was emptied into their troughs and all would be quiet. Bert would reappear with the empty bucket, refilling it to carry off food to another lot of noisy pigs.

Soon the rattle of milking pails and buckets being washed in the dairy was heard, only for them to be stored away ready for the morning milk. Massey the waggoner, having fed the horse, would come to the back door to collect his can of milk. With a "Goodnight all," he would disappear down the yard on his way home, with his snap bag hanging from his shoulder, can in hand and smoke coming from his pipe. I wondered why he didn't come into the house like my brothers when he collected his milk can. On asking my father why, he replied in a firm voice, "He's only a workman." This made me think and puzzled my mind, for, to me, he was a man just the same as my father and brothers. To make things worse, Father didn't take the time to explain to me why some people are workmen and others masters, for they all worked equally hard on the farm.

My sister and brothers would now start coming in for tea. The rattling buckets had become silent. The animals were fed. We would all sit around the table. The hanging paraffin lamp reflected shadows over the table, which was loaded with food like home-made bread, jam and cheese. Sometimes, there would be thick slices of fat home-cured boiled bacon.

The evening meal was finished. The conversation had been as it always was, about what had gone on during the day, what cow was going to calve during the night or what they had seen the neighbours doing.

Mother and Muriel would do the washing up, for by now the maid had gone home. Brother Harold would give a hand with washing eggs, which had been collected during the day in bucketfuls. As the eggs were packed away they were checked for cracks, size and colour, for it was the time in the year, February, when they were selected for hatching in the incubators. Also, neighbours around our farm would call in for eggs.

Soon work was done and the dark had closed in around the farm. I often stood looking up into the darkness at the moon and stars. Perhaps Mother would sing about the man in the moon and the cow that jumped over the moon. Some cow, I thought. I would ask, "How does the man get into the moon?" "With a ladder," came the reply. Soon, Mother would tire of my questions and talk about me going to bed. I would pretend not to hear, still looking through the window to catch sight of Bert's lamp as he was taking a last look around the animals for the night. This was known as 'supping up'.

The fire in the range would now be burning bright and warm. The mat had been placed over the stone floor in front of the fire. During the day it was rolled up and put aside so that the clogs would not wear it out. Father would be sitting in a corner to one side reading the *Daily Mail*. Mother would draw up the wooden chair, sit by the fire and take out her hairpins, unrolling her long hair which had during the day been tied in a bun at the back of her head. Harold and Muriel would be sitting at the table knitting and making daily notes with one eye on Father to see when he was finished with the newspaper. Cyril would be doing his homework. When all was settled and I thought Mother had forgotten about me going to bed, Father would suddenly say, half-looking over his paper, "Mother, isn't it about time you got that young'un up to bed, and stop his chatter so I can get some peace?"

At this Mother would turn around to look across at Muriel, saying, "Take the lad to bed."

Muriel seemed to accept her instructions. She would go into the pantry for the little Kelly lamp, bringing a biscuit or two which I would nibble to delay 'going up the wooden hills' to bed. Eventually Father would throw the paper down onto his knees, exclaiming, "Mother, get that child to bed!"

Muriel immediately gathered me up with the light as well and up the wooden stairs we went. Soon I was tucked down in my feather bed and sleep overtook me.

Morning seemed to come so soon. As I lay in the warm bed I could hear the sound of the morning work being done, smell the bacon being cooked in the kitchen below. There were voices as people went about their various tasks and dogs barking at the cattle as they crossed the yard on the way to the field.

One morning, when I got out of the warm bed and went over to the window that overlooked the orchard and the fields beyond, I could see Mother letting the fowl out of the pens. As she opened the shutter the hens rushed out, necks outstretched, wings flapping as if they were glad to be out. The cockerel flapped his big wings, looked up at the sky with his neck outstretched and crowed his head off as if to tell the world "I am up, I am up!" I watched him run a hen around the orchard until he caught her. This excited me. Then I went downstairs to the kitchen to find a bright warm fire and breakfast being prepared. Mother came in with a bowl of water and a cloth and towel. I knew it was my time to get washed and dressed. I wondered why the cockerel chased the hens like he did.

During breakfast I asked, "Why does the cockerel run the hens around the orchard?"

Looking round the table I could see different expressions on the faces of those seated there, as if I had knocked over the jam pot. No one said a word; they just looked at each other.

"Why?" I asked again.

Mother, with firmness in her voice, said, "You want to know too much. Be quiet at the table!"

End of question time.

Breakfast over and my coat on, I went out into the orchard to my stick animals, which were still laid out behind the wall. I placed grass in front of them just as I had seen the cattle fed. When I was a little older, I would place them out in the orchard as if they were in fields. I became very involved in this make-believe farming. Those sticks became so real.

Then I wandered into the cattle sheds where Bert and Harold were cleaning out the muck, wheeling each barrow onto the muckheap behind the building. I loved to help brush up the floors. Harold carried in clean straw from the stackyard, breaking the string tying each straw bale together. He shook it to form a nice clean bed for the cows when they came in later that day.

Now the call for dinner could be heard. Stopping what we were doing, we made our way across the yard to the house. Because I was a thumb-sucker, my right thumb was always white clean when I came to wash my hands, even when they were dirty from helping in the cattle sheds.

During the morning, Muriel had brought her cycle to the house. I can see that cycle now. It was a lady's 'sit up and beg' model with big wheels and very high handlebars. It had a string-like cord stretched and arranged in a fan shape from the back mudguard to the spindle of the rear wheel to prevent the long dresses getting caught in the spokes. Seeing the cycle leaning against the house wall reminded me that I was going to see my grandmother and grandfather.

CHAPTER TWO

Visiting my grandparents

After dinner, Muriel brought my best clothes over by the kitchen fire; also, a sponge and a bowl of warm water. Then she started getting me ready for my outing. I hated being washed and dressed up like a 'dog's dinner' but it had to be. Muriel and I, in our Sunday best, set off on our journey to Lockley Wood four miles north west of the farm, with me sitting on the metal carrier, hanging on to her coat with both hands. She pedalled away on our journey, travelling past the open common land. When we arrived at the gate of Grandma's garden, she lifted me off the seat and fussed with my clothes and woolly bonnet, then she opened the gate and we went up the path to the front door with its shining brass knocker and handles.

As we both walked up the neatly-bordered path I noticed for the first time a huge monkey puzzle tree. It stood so tall with its branches arranged like large monkey tails hanging low down to the ground. Fascinated with this tree, I did not see Grandma standing in the doorway to welcome us.

Entering the house I became aware of the dark wood panelling in the hall; also, the smell that went with that type of decoration and varnished wallpaper. Grandma led the way down the hallway towards the living room. She was a stately figure, her grey hair neatly rolled into a bun which I could see under the pure white bonnet that was tied with a bow under her chin. The dress was long and black with large black buttons in the middle of her waist, and hanging down to the ground so that you could only see the tips of her black shoes. When I got into the living room, she turned to take off my coat. As she did so, I saw the long white frills edging her black dress. I thought the expression on her face was just like my mother's – firm and perhaps a little hard, with eyes that seemed to peer right through you.

Grandfather was beside the fireplace, his greying hair and beard lit up from the glow of the log fire which burnt in the grate. Grandfather felt warm and reassuring, for as I walked over to him he put his outstretched arms on my shoulders. I could feel the gentle touch of his hands become firm as he lifted me onto his knee. I gazed into his face – the beard, his eyes seeming to express his joy and happiness to have me on his knees. Soon, I relaxed in the room. Things within it became real, and although I'd been there on many occasions before, this felt like the first time. I began to remember and question what the things were, as if to learn about them.

Sitting warm and secure on Grandfather's lap, I looked around the room. At the same time, Grandfather tore strips from the daily newspaper, placing them in his long fingers and rolling each piece into a spill, which he would place in a tin on the hob, until they were required to light his pipe or the lamps at night. Down on the floor beside him, I could see a bundle of newspapers torn into pieces about four inches square. Looking down at these I asked, "Grandpa, what are those pieces of paper for?"

With a rye smile on his face he replied, "Bum fodder!"

"What's bum fodder, Grandfather?"

Before he could say, Grandma, on her rocking chair opposite, said, "William, do not fill that child's head with such rubbish!" – giving an extra rock as she sat in her chair.

He pulled me close to him, whispering, "Never mind, in

trouble yet again! We'll have a pipe of baccy."

His hand shuffled around his coat pocket, bringing out a tin, together with his white clay pipe, the bowl blackened. Laying the pipe down on the hob and opening the tin, he took out a piece of twist tobacco and placing it in the palms of his hands rubbed it until it broke up into small pieces, which he carefully packed into his clay pipe. Occasionally he put it to his mouth for a preliminary check to make sure he had not packed the tobacco too tightly. After replacing the lid on his tin and returning it to his pocket, he reached over to the hob, took one of his paper spills, lit it from the fire, then raised and placed it over the pipe's bowl. A few quick puffs and smoke was all around me. Satisfied that the pipe was well alight he tapped the smouldering paper spill out in the fire.

With a smile of contentment he leaned back into the wooden armchair and held me close to his warm chest. I could hear the watch in his breast jacket pocket, quietly ticking away. As puffs of smoke came through his grey beard, I asked, " Why doesn't your whiskers burn, Grandpa?"

With a chuckle in his voice he replied, "You see boy, when I puffs the smoke out, I blows 'em out..."

I put out my hand to touch his beard to see if it was hot. As he puffed, the smoke and smell filled the living room. At the same time I blew out my cheeks just as Grandpa did. Seeing me do this he reached over to a shelf where his new pipes were, and put one in my mouth as if I was smoking too.

"William!" came a retort in a very loud voice from Grandmother, "You'll make the boy sick, teaching him your dirty habits."

A pause.

"Shut up, woman. Let the boy enjoy himself."

A silence followed. As I looked peacefully around the room, my eyes focused on the tall grandfather clock, which reached up to the low-beamed ceiling. I listened to the deep regular note as it ticked the minutes away and noticed the painted face on a small dial showing a shape of the moon.

"How does that work, Grandpa?" I asked.

He did his best to explain, but in the end he promised to show me inside the clock. When he got up my eyes gazed further around the room. Above me on the mantelshelf were placed two china dogs and brass candleholders, together with odd pieces of paper. Around the front of the shelf was draped a cloth with a fringe matching the one covering the table in the middle of the room. Over the table, hanging from the ceiling by four chains, was a brass-framed paraffin lamp. The base containing paraffin was of glass and the fuel could easily be seen. Across the room in the bay windows was a big aspidistra plant hanging from a tall stand, which seemed to block out most of the light. By the side of the fire, where the brass fire irons were, was a brass buttonhook which was used daily by Grandma to button her ankle-length boots. As we sat, Grandpa's pipe had gone out.

I wanted to go and see outside. Soon Grandpa put on his flat cap, which had been hanging on the back of his chair. Then taking from his pocket a large red handkerchief with small white spots all over it, he wiped his face and said, "Let's go and feed the animals." For in the small fields and garden he kept three or four young calves and some hens. I asked Grandpa why he didn't have lots and lots of hens and cows as my father had. His reply was that they cost a lot of pennies.

His work done, Grandpa and I returned into the house. As we entered the living room on the table I could see a big cake on a stand and the cups for tea set out. Muriel pulled up the chair to the table and placed me near to Grandpa. As Grandma poured out the tea for the three of them I had to have some home-made lemonade. Muriel cut the cake, passing us all a portion each. I couldn't wait for Grandpa to start eating so I could get on with mine. I liked Grandma's fruit-cake, but I hated the home-made lemonade for it had bits and pieces in it. Grandpa, seeing I did not like drinking it, asked for some bread and cheese, then whilst Grandma was out of the room he poured some of his tea into his saucer. He offered it to my lips and I sipped it quickly. Just as the saucer was being returned to the cup, Grandma came back with the cheese. With her eyes fixed, she said, "William, you haven't been giving that child tea?"

"No, no," replied Grandpa, pretending to wipe his mouth with his red handkerchief.

Grandma questioned Muriel again, but with a straight face she said that she had not been taking notice.

When we had finished, Muriel looked up to the clock, saying, "It's time that we were going."

Soon I was dressed and placed on my seat on the cycle. As Grandfather bent down to say goodbye, I declared, "I like you, Grandpa!"

With a warm smile on his face, he patted me on the head and turned to Muriel, saying, "Get that lad home and safe."

Soon we turned the corner on our way.

The afternoon sun had set behind us. I could feel the chill wind on my knees as Muriel pedalled. The occasional rabbit dashed from the hedgerow and blackbirds flew along the hedges in front of us giving out their evening chirp – for this was the time of day when their thoughts were on finding a warm place to sleep. As we passed between the common land I heard the call of a cock pheasant in the undergrowth. He was collecting his last tasty morsels of the day. Muriel told me about how he would be going to sleep in his favourite holly bush, sleeping as high as he could get to protect him-self from the wandering fox. Suddenly a fear came over me. With a squeak in my voice I asked, "Will the fox get me?"

"No, my pet," was the reply. This reassured me.

When the home farm was in sight we saw our neighbour's horses walking towards us. As they came near I heard the click-click of their steel shoes coming into contact with the gravel road, the chains on their harness swinging to and fro as they took each stride. The long white hair on their legs was all muddy and soil hung from it like cricket balls. I noticed the waggoner leading the horses towards us; his slow measured step was in time with those of the horses, for they had all had a long day ploughing in the field nearby. As they passed the waggoner touched his cap. At the same time in a deep voice he said, "Good day Miss and to you Master."

Muriel acknowledged his welcome: "Same to you, Bates."

She pedalled on. As the sound of the horses faded I tried to turn and look back but I was soon told to sit still as I was making the cycle wobble.

We turned down the drive home. I could see Rover standing wagging his tail and with a few quick barks he welcomed us home again. As we crossed the cow yard, I could see milking had started. Muriel pushed the cycle into the small house yard. After leaning the cycle against the house she lifted me down. By this time I was so cold and my legs were so stiff that I found it hard to walk. Realising my feelings, Muriel gathered me up in her arms and took me into the warm kitchen. Soon standing in front of the hot fire I was my old self again. Muriel stood beside me warming her hands, then took off her hat and coat, and also mine. Suddenly Mother came in through the door without a word of enquiry about Grandma or whether I had enjoyed myself. Looking hard at Muriel she said, "You are late. They have been milking for half an hour now. The sooner you get out there to help the better."

Then as Mother went back into the scullery muttering to herself about being late, Muriel turned to me and saying not a word walked across the kitchen, hung up my clothes on the peg and went upstairs to change.

The way Mother had shouted made me cry for I had so much to tell her about Grandpa and my journey. It seemed that she didn't want to know. The milking and work were more important. My feelings meant nothing to her at the moment.

Muriel soon came down into the kitchen. I had sat myself on a stool in front of the fire, tears rolling down my face. I felt as if no one wanted me. Muriel stood by me, "Come on, my pet, please don't cry."

As she reassured me, Mother came back in.

"Don't fuss him. Get out to that milking!"

Muriel swung round.

"To hell with the milking," she said, as she pulled on her milking cap.

Mother's face turned white with anger and with a dish-cloth in her hand she followed Muriel out of the kitchen.

Soon Mother returned, leaving the door into the scullery open. Going over to the sideboard drawer she took out the tablecloth, slamming it down onto the table. Then she turned to the dresser. Out came the cups, saucers and plates, they too went hard down on the table. I heard Harold tipping buckets of milk into the cheese vat. Mother looked through the scullery door and shouted, "Don't slop that milk about, I just cleaned the floor."

She returned towards me.

"Don't sit there sniffling, move yourself."

I quickly shuffled myself into a corner well out of her way, for when she was in these moods no one was safe.

Mealtime was a quiet occasion that evening. Also, it was early to bed for me. As Muriel put me in the bed, tucking the bedclothes in tight, I remembered Grandpa had not shown me inside the big clock as he promised.

"Never mind, he will the next time we go," she told me.

"Why is Mother so angry?"

"Don't worry, go to sleep. She will be all right in the morning."

CHAPTER THREE

Lambing

The days passed, cheese and butter making went on the same as in the weeks before. February that year had been a month of sunshine, rain and snow. Father would make a comment about the days getting longer. This was a time of preparation and expectation for the much talked-about new lambs arriving. In the barn hurdles were place to make small pens. Straw was tied to the sides and a covering placed over the top, making a warm little house for the ewe and her new lambs. I loved helping with this work.

Father lifted me into the float and with a "Come on Rover!" in jumped the dog and soon we were trotting up the lane towards the field where the ewes were waiting for their daily feed. As Dolly walked over the field all the sheep followed behind us. Father stopped the pony and float beside the feeding troughs. Getting down he walked over to the troughs and began to load each one onto the float. All on, he tied the hayrack to the back of the float. The sheep all seemed quite put out about such goings on; no food. All this time Rover was not allowed out of the float because Father did not want the ewes running about. When everything was on board and we were ready to go home came the moment that Rover was waiting for. As he circled the sheep Father gave him instructions in a clear voice. Soon the sheep were walking slowly through the gate turning towards home.

Quietly down the lane we proceeded. Sitting on the seat in the float and turning back, I looked at the sheep quietly walking behind. Rover's eyes seemed to be watching every ewe. Father walked on, knowing that Rover would do his job. Soon we arrived at a field near the farm buildings. Turning into the field the sheep followed close behind. The pony stopped. Soon the troughs were being laid out in a row. Then the bags of food were emptied out. Hay was placed in the rack and Rover popped up into the float and sat beside me.

As the sheep tucked into their food, Father walked behind them looking closely at each and every one. All done, we returned to the farmyard. Dolly was tied up by the haystack to await the next task. The ewes had been brought to this particular field to enable them to be watched from the house when the lambs started to arrive.

While we had dinner Mother wanted to know all about the sheep and what condition they were in. I just had to tell her about what we had done and for once she seemed to listen to what I had to tell.

While we were at dinner it had started to rain. This meant I had to stay in the house. Fortunately, Mother was getting the incubators ready for hatching eggs. I liked going down into the cellar, which was four or five steps down from the kitchen. Around the walls at one end were rows of shelves on which home-made jams, pickles and apples were stored. Hanging from hooks in the ceiling were the sides of bacon and cured hams. Low down were the cold slate settles where butter and cream were kept.

The incubator was at the other end, away from the stores. Mother gave me a cloth to dry off the egg trays, which had been washed. When I had dried off the trays she put them back into the incubator. The next thing to be done was to check the damper controls and the wicks of the lamps. All this done, she would light up the final setting of the damper and the incubator would be brought up to the right temperature ready for the eggs in a few days.

By now the rainwater was running down the yard. As I watched through the window I could see Bert feeding the pigs. On top of his overcoat he had put a meal sack over his shoulders, like a cape, to keep himself dry. In the orchard the fowl were looking wet and miserable, sheltering under the trees and hedges. No matter what the weather is like, on farms work has to go on just the same.

Soon everyone was coming in for the evening meal. I could see wet clothes hanging around and on the boiler in the scullery. Everyone seemed to be fed up.

The evening was spent just as many evenings before.

Next day I was up early to see if the new lambs had arrived – running out to the pens we had put up the day before and looking in. To my disappointment there were no lambs. Why, when the grown-ups said that this was what would happen?

During breakfast I asked Father why he hadn't put the new lambs in the pen.

He replied, "Perhaps tomorrow or the next day."

"Why? You said 'tomorrow', yesterday."

They will never come, I thought.

The morning was spent around the building, as always. That afternoon I can remember helping Mother fill the incubator with eggs. While we were doing this she noticed a neighbour coming down the yard with a basket on his arm. Mother met him at the door.

"Mr Cork, what brings you here? Come in and take a seat."

I can remember standing by the kitchen table looking at him. As he sat down on the wooden chair he took off his bowler hat. It was a very funny shape, round with a narrow brim. I thought it looked like a chamber pot without a handle as it lay on the floor beside him. He chatted on whilst Mother was busy packing the eggs he had come over for. At that moment Father came into the kitchen.

"Hello, Fred, what are you wanting?"

"A few sitting eggs for my incubator."

As they were talking I stood by the table looking at his face and his pointed nose. Around his neck was a silk scarf crossing over his chest and tucked into his corded waistcoat. His big boots seemed too heavy for his little legs.

Looking over at me he said, "That lad's growing. Soon he will be going to school, eh?"

"Not 'til the end of the year," came the reply.

"Have you been keeping well, Fred?"

"Not too bad. I am a bit like the church fleas. Getting a good meal on a Sunday." He smiled at this remark.

After a short pause, Mother said, "I hear you had the hounds in the wood by you?"

"Oh ah. They didn't find a fox. Oh ah. Did you hear about old Jack Cartwright?"

"Now what?" asked Mother. "What's happened, Fred?"

"It's like this. Jack had been with the hounds and as they left the wood he went behind that old barn for a leak." He was half telling this tale and laughing.

"Come Fred, tell us."

"Well it was like this. He went behind the barn for a leak. Lo and behold, her ladyship from the Hall was off her horse with her britches down. I believe Jack didn't know what to do. So he touched his cap and stuttering like a ferret said, 'Sorry ma'am', turned on his heels and left her there. They say old Jack's face was like a bloody beetroot. He'll never live that down. And the best of it was that she came from behind the barn walking the horse over and asking whether Cartwright could give her a leg up. Well, what could he do? Then, as she rode off she said, 'It is surprising what you see,

Hinstock Grange, pictured when it was the home of the Dilworth family

Father (left) and the farm hands

Above: Victor as a young man

Left: Mother feeding the hens

*Right:
Mother and
Father outside
the front door
of Hinstock
Grange*

Cartwright, when you are out hunting.'"

Now the eggs had been packed, on went his hat and shuffling his hands in his trouser pocket he brought out the money for the eggs. As he went down the yard I can remember to this day his short bow-legs going into those big boots. Mother put on her working overcoat and went outside to feed the hens, collecting more eggs as she went.

Lizzie, the other maid, came in the kitchen to do some ironing. I could not resist showing her how Mr Cork walked. I put on a pair of boots and walked across the kitchen just as I had seen Mr Cork going down the yard. She laughed so much she burnt herself with the iron.

During the evening, the main conversation was about Mr Cork and what he had told us. I also repeated my imitations of him.

The following morning, as I took a peep through the bedroom window I could see the sheep grazing. Then, all of a sudden, Harold came in sight carrying something in his hands with a sheep following close behind. I became more and more excited, putting my thumb in my mouth as if to steady my nerves. As he came near I realised he was carrying two little lambs. Soon I was chasing down the stairs so that I could get dressed quickly and go out to see. Mother as usual was going about her morning tasks and would not leave whatever she was doing. I was so wanting to see the new lambs. I must have worried her so much but it was soon clear that she would not leave the job at hand so that I could get dressed as quickly as I wanted. Eventually, she made time to attend to me. But still I had to have my breakfast before being let outside. Soon Harold got my outdoor clothes on me, promising to let me see the lambs. This was the first time I could really remember lambs being born. The excitement was something that I had not experienced before. As Harold opened the pen I saw this small animal lying in the clean straw with its mother standing over it protectively. As he lifted it from the straw bed I became frightened – perhaps 'withdrawn' is a better way of putting it – as it was not what I had expected. For the lamb's legs just hung down like a rag doll's, and its skin was wrinkled like a woollen jersey which was many times too big.

I put my hand carefully on its head and as my hand came into contact with it the feeling was very difficult to put into words. I found it repulsive for it was wet and sticky, not like the woollier cuddly animal I had seen in the picture books. I recall my disappointment. Harold, seeing that I was frightened, returned the lamb to its mother, who immediately started licking the little creature all over as it stood on those wobbly legs.

All that morning I played about the building. I could not help but think about the lamb, going back to peep into the pen. As the day passed I began to accept the idea of holding the little lamb for by now he had become a little white woolly bundle. His ears, nose and legs all had black patches on them. I loved to watch him try to jump about. Then he would fall over. Again and again he got back up onto his legs, which seemed far too long for the size of his body. Then he would tuck his head under his mother's belly. Soon he was wagging his little tail. While I was peeping in, Father came up to see if all was well, bringing hay, corn and water for the mother. Seeing the lamb in the pen, all I wanted to do was hold it. So I pushed in beside my father, reaching out to touch the lamb. To my surprise it was now warm and soft – not what I had experienced earlier that morning.

The days, then weeks had passed. Mother had tended the eggs in the incubator, damping them with water and turning them every day. Lambs had been arriving fast. Every one of the family seemed to be involved in the newborn animals.

To me it was a time for thought and excitement, for I had seen the lambs born, heard them make their first sound, stand for the first time on their wobbly legs, fall over and try again until their first steps took them towards their mothers' side. I would sit nearby to watch them push their little heads under their mother's belly searching for the teats. This was so important for the lamb to survive. Soon contact with the teat would be made. The lamb's tail would shake from side to side and its mother would lick its back, making a noise in her throat as if she was excited and proud of her baby. Then there were times when sadly I came up against death, for lambs and their mothers would die. This gave everyone a feeling of sadness but not despair, for I remember Father – as big as he was – looking down on the dead animals, pushing his hat back on his head and saying, "Oh well, it can't be helped. The Lord won't let us win every time."

Then he would take me by the hand to walk away and look at the lambs that were skipping about on the grass in the field.

Soon I began to understand that life and death are part of life, and that there is no label on any one of us when we are born to say when we will die. We only have the will we are given to survive, so that we can blossom and mature, then reseed, recreating life like the flowers, the great trees and the smallest animals and birds on the earth. There is no difference – we all eat and strive to grow, and then die – but when and how no one knows, nor what happens in the years between. No matter if we are kings or the smallest creature it comes to nothing, yet we all have to, whilst living, maintain life so that we make the most of it. Mother always said, "One must earn his crust, body will turn to dust, but memories take a long time to rust."

Over a lifetime I have come to realise that all creatures on earth are dependent on each other, just like the strands of a spider's web suspended on a hedgerow in autumn.

After being with Father around the farm I always turned to my world of stick animals in the farmyard, and I would throw one away as if it had died. I made small sticks as lambs. This was my real world.

Around the dinner table all the conversation was about the newborn animals and the extra work that my brothers had to do. It was times like this when I would want to sit on my mother's lap for a cuddle and the reassurance of love but she would reject me, saying, "I haven't the time to nurse you now." So I would find myself sitting on the stool by the fire sucking my thumb.

Everybody was rushing around; the noise of their clogs on the hard floors; the swish of water; the pump handle being pushed up and down as they were scrubbing out the dairy. But even with all this going on around me I was lonely. I would sit looking into the fire dreaming of what I would like to be when I grew up. As the fire faded my eyes would become sleepy. Soon I would get up onto the long wooden bench behind the table, putting the cushion on which I sat at mealtimes under my head, and curling up to sleep for a while. Very often I was awakened by the noise of someone rattling the poker on the range as they made the fire up or wanting to sweep or scrub the kitchen floor. I began to hate being disturbed in this way. In my child's mind I felt – perhaps 'rejected' is the wrong word – but lost, and that the noise and work was more important. That was all grown-ups did. But I was too small to take part.

Mother would come in on her way to look at the eggs in the incubator, for now it was time for the hatching to begin. As she opened the door of the incubator I could see a little chick and beside it the two halves of a shell. Other eggs were being cracked. Mother would take an egg in her hand and hold it by my ear so that I could hear the little chicken inside tapping on the shell to get out.

After seeing all was well with the hatching and checking on the temperature, Mother would leave the cellar to go about other work. But not me. I would stand what seemed like hours looking through the window into the hatching eggs. It was just low enough for my eye level and enabled me to see well into the tray of eggs. As I watched a particular egg I saw a small crack appear. Watching more intently after a while a beak could be seen pushing and chipping away at the shell. As the hole got larger the chick's head started to appear. Then after a lot of pushing the eggshell seemed to fall into two pieces revealing the tiny chick wet and exhausted. After a short while, I noticed the little tiny newborn lift its head to look at its new surroundings. Its eyes blinked again and again as if the light was too bright. Soon a little yellow leg unfolded from under its body, pushing onto the open shell and freeing itself with every movement.

Then all of a sudden, it rolled out of the shell which had been its home. As it lay looking to me, exhausted after its fight and struggle to emerge into the wide open space, I wanted to open the door so that I could take hold of the tiny thing. But this I could not do, for Mother had already smacked my legs for opening the incubator door weeks previously, threatening me with the cow strap if I did it again. This frightened me for I had seen her use it on my brother Cyril before, and I remember to this day how he cried.

Muriel came in to fetch me to help her with getting in the sticks and coal in for next morning's fire-lighting. As I was telling her about seeing the lambs and chicks being born I asked her whether I was born like that, calling Muriel by her nickname 'Moo-Moo'.

"I don't know," came the reply.

"Why?" I asked again. Then after we had filled the buckets with coal and Muriel had packed a bundle of sticks into my arms I looked up into her face.

"Moo-Moo, if you put me in an incubator, would I hatch little men?"

Before I had finished what I was going to say she burst into laughter.

"Oh my darling, where do you get such ideas? God makes all little ones."

"Did he make me?"

Soon we were back in the house and I was told to be quiet.

"You want to know too much."

I often look back on those early days, realising how lucky I was to see and be part of all this going on around me and not being protected from the hard facts of life. This is something many children born to a town environment never experience, for their parents seem to protect them from living and dying and they do not have the opportunity to share life with animals and pets.

By now I was in my father's eyes big enough to do more little jobs of fetching and carrying. One morning, breakfast finished, he said, "I have a job for you this morning, young man. Mind some pigs." For father had to send some fat pigs to the bacon factory and a lorry would be collecting them during the morning.

A big loose box was strawed down to keep the pigs clean. In those days pigs were fattened in their family groups in individual sties. This meant that Father selected the fattest pig from every litter, then put them all together in the prepared loose box. My job on these occasions was to sit in a corner on a milking stool holding a stick, so if the pigs started fighting I had to run amongst them hitting them with the stick to stop them. Father liked the pigs to arrive at the factory clean and in prime condition. I am sure reading this you can imagine a small boy, barely four years old, running among perhaps ten or twenty pigs of bacon weight with a stick. I was always small in height yet I did it without fear, nor did anyone realise the danger I could have been in. Sometimes, the lorry was early, other times not so early. As the last pig ran up into the lorry I would think myself a big boy now.

The year went on, the sun got warmer; seeds were being sown in the fields and I was going to bed in daylight, which was something I hated. The lambs and chicks I had seen born had grown much bigger and the cows were being turned out into the fields.

Muriel would take me up the lane. The setting sun would throw shadows on the hedgerows and as we wandered she would show me the wild flowers growing in the hedge banks. Occasionally, I would pick a primrose and other pretty flowers. As we strolled the birds were giving out their evening songs and the little wrens could be seen searching for insects. Cows would stop grazing to look over the hedge to see what we were doing. You had a feeling that all the animals were happy and excited to share this warm Spring evening. Soon we'd turn to make our way back to the house only to see the dog had wandered up the lane behind us, for he loved to search in the grassy banks for the mice that ventured out of their burrows. One particular evening I can remember listening to the church bells as the bell-ringers practised their art.

A walk in a country lane in late evening following a hot day always brings back to me some of the happy times of my childhood.

CHAPTER FOUR

Sundays

My early memories of Sundays are of a day of inactivity with a lot of do's and don'ts. The only jobs done about the farm were the necessary ones like milking the cows and feeding the poultry and pigs. The milk was stored in the vats, for even cheese-making was not done until the next day, Monday.

The main thing to feel excited about was lunchtime, for Mother would roast the joint of beef which I had seen the butcher deliver on Saturday morning. Along with the roast would be extra baked potatoes that had been cooked around the meat. Often I would see Mother baste the meat and potatoes with the hot fat. Oh, what a lovely smell, roasting meat together with the rest of the Sunday lunch. For me, nothing can replace the atmosphere of food being cooked in a farmhouse kitchen range. The hot fire, the steam from the boiling pots; seeing Mother in a white apron all stiff and starched, attending to and watching over the cooking. This was one of the times when she seemed to be relaxed and have the time to talk to me. She would tell me stories of her childhood and how my Grandma had taught her all about cooking and how Grandpa had grown all the vegetables in his garden. She was another mother from the person I experienced on weekdays, when she was all hard and rushing about. I sometimes wished for Sundays every day.

As the food was finally prepared Muriel would be setting

the table. This was the day when the newly-washed and starched tablecloth would be brought out. As she carefully flattened it out she would remind all present not to drop any food on the cloth as it had got to last all week. I would help in laying the knives and forks around the table and the place mats would come out, something that was not used in the week. The plates and dishes would all be put onto the long plate rack over the range to warm. Soon, Father and my brothers could be heard in the scullery washing their hands, chatting about what they had done. In the week this did not happen, for they came in at intervals, all rushing, but today, Sunday, all would come into the kitchen together with Father leading the way. They were all clean with their faces bright and fresh, and their hair damped with water as they combed some kind of parting. Their week's growth of whiskers had been shaved off. They all put on their tidy clothes and clean shirts. I often thought to myself, "Why do they do this on Sundays and not other days?"

When everyone was seated around the table Father would take up the carving knife and steel, as if it was a ritual to sharpen the knife before cutting the joint which Mother had placed in front of him on the table. Everyone's eyes seemed focused on the meat, all brown and piping hot. Father would always cut off the first slice, placing it to one side of the great meat dish, then he would cut slice after slice, placing them carefully on each of the dinner plates. Soon they were being passed around. Sometimes the meat would be a little fat; very often I would wish my slice would be lean. After everyone had taken their baked potatoes, vegetables and a portion of Yorkshire pudding – of which I would always like a corner piece – and Mother had taken her place at the table, we would start eating the meal.

Sundays came and went and I began to wonder why Father always placed the first slice of meat to the side of the meat dish, then as he finished carving and the dish was about to be taken away, he would slide this slice onto his own plate. So one day I thought I would ask him why.

"Father, why do you always have the first piece of meat?"

"Oh, you see, it is all burnt and you would not like it."

"Why, you like it, so why can't I?"

Immediately the tone of his voice changed and everyone around the table came to a deathly hush. I realised it was time to drop the subject.

After the meat and two vegetables there was always apple or some other fruit pie, the crust all nice and crisp, for the pies were made on Sunday for the week. The difference was that in the week they were always served cold and sometimes with lumpy custard. The pastry was thick and tasteless and I hated it. But I liked my Sunday pies.

Sunday was a day of rest for it was wrong to sew or darn socks, work the horses, or listen to the radio – we were only allowed to sit and be quiet. Some Sunday evenings we would put on our Sunday best and visit Grandma or friends, but I remember one particular Sunday when my Uncle Harry and Aunty Gertie were coming over for tea. This meant tea would be taken in the large dining room and not in the kitchen. The dining room was kept spick and span but was little used. The floor was of red tiles polished so much that it was like walking on an ice pond. In the centre of the room was the large mahogany table which you could extend to seat about fifteen to twenty people. When you placed a handle at the end of a frame under the table top and cranked away, the table would open up to expose extra leaves. Around the table were the dining chairs. These had very upright backs and cold leather seats. I hated them. My poor little legs got very cold because I wore very short trousers.

The large window overlooked the tennis court and gardens. In the far distance you could see the Wrekin and the outlines of the Welsh mountains. In the fields immediately beyond the garden one would, in summer, see the cattle grazing amongst the wild flowers, buttercups and daisies growing in the garden hedgerow and the blossom of the damson and apple trees. On an occasional evening you would see, in the evening light, a fox wandering his way across the meadow. The cattle would lift their heads looking at him passing. The plovers flew overhead, swooping down low as if this would frighten the fox and make him pass more quickly. On Sundays Father would watch: had it been a weekday he would have reached for his gun to chase this intruder away, but on Sunday guns should not be fired.

I must tell you about the arrival of my uncle and aunt for I had been washed and dressed in my Sunday clothes. My shoes were polished and my socks pulled up showing no wrinkles – for they were held up just below the knee by elastic bands which cut into my legs until they left red marks. Muriel and Mother had put on their best frocks. Mother had also put on her rings and silver brooch. "Eh, they looked real posh!" Muriel gave the room a final flick with a duster. Father had put on his country tweed suit. You could see his gold watch chain across the front of his waistcoat. As he sat reading the church magazine he would from time to time make appropriate remarks to Mother about something he had read. I was playing with the wooden jigsaw puzzle of a black and white cow. I had done this puzzle so many times before that it was a bore to play with. I would have much preferred to have gone on the tennis court with a bat and ball but I couldn't because it was Sunday.

The dog barked to announce the arrival of my uncle in his Rover car. Father went into the yard to welcome them in, and Mother followed close behind. Muriel and I were expected to stay in the house, for children in the early 1920s were to be seen but not heard. My brothers had vanished into the farm buildings to return only when tea was about to begin.

Uncle was not a tall man, but not short. Like my father, he was dressed in a heavy tweed suit. He always had a brown trilby hat which he removed as he shook hands with Mother and Father. His face was of a ruddy complexion and down the side were long whiskers, the like of which I had only seen in books portraying Mister Pickwick. His voice was soft and reassuring. As for Aunty Gertie, my mother's sister, she was much taller and of a heavy build. Her manner was that of a 'country lady' and her dress was of style and quality. I can remember the round straw hat perched on her head, displaying on one side a bunch of flowers and secured with a pearl hatpin. Draped on her shoulders was an animal fur stole and from around her neck a row of pearls hung low down on her chest. On the long black dress she wore a lace handkerchief.

As they entered the house you felt my aunt's eyes going through you and also passing around the room to see if it had been dusted. They handed their coats and hats to Muriel and Aunty, in a haughty voice, remarked, "Nellie, that boy's growing up. You should get his hair cut better."

"Yes, Gertie," came Mother's reply.

As Gertie passed me by she pulled my coat open to look if my neck and shirt were clean. I did not like Aunty very much. Uncle was so different. He was gentle, for he talked to me, asking what I liked doing and listening to every word I said.

As they went into the sitting room across the hall from the dining room, Muriel continued with the laying of the dining table. The best silver knives and spoons were taken from the long sideboard where they had been wrapped up in soft cloth. The fine bone china tea service was also placed neatly on the table. I was always impressed by the three-tier silver cake stand, full of delicate home-made cakes. Bread and butter was cut thinly into triangular pieces, not like the thick square slices we had normally. At the end of the table where Father sat was a large joint of home-made ham, which had been rolled in brown bread crumbs. Mother came in the dining room to see if everything was in its place. This was one of the many childhood memories I never forgot – a table delightfully dressed and the late afternoon sun streaming in through the window, casting reflections and shadows on the silver cutlery and white napkins rolled into their silver rings.

From time to time my brothers popped into the kitchen to see if tea was ready and at the same time grab a handful of bread crusts which had been cut off the bread and butter. Although Aunt and Uncle were visiting, the work outside like milking and feeding animals continued just the same. But by now everything was ready; Muriel told Cyril to tell my other brothers to get washed and tidy.

Father, Uncle and Aunty came into the dining room to stand at their places around the table and shake hands with other members of the family they had not met when arriving. Everyone in, Father invited Uncle to take his seat. As he sat we all followed, taking our napkins from the side plates and placing them on our laps. I was considered too small to do this. I had to have mine placed around my neck and tied at the back. Under my plate was a small cloth to stop me marking the tablecloth. Father carved the ham, passing the plates and portions around the table. Soon everyone had taken his or her salads. Muriel had carried in the silver teapot and sat down in the vacant chair beside me. Mother poured the tea but not for me. It was then considered bad for children. I had to be satisfied with orange juice. Soon the conversation got down to the boring old subject of animals, cheese-making and what the unemployed people were doing or not doing. As for me, not being able or allowed to join in the conversations, I had soon eaten my food and had to sit quietly while the grown-ups chatted and slowly munched away. Mother enquired whether Gertie required more tea.

"More tea?" I thought. "I wish she'd choke!"

I could feel her eyes on me and my brothers, watching to see if they held their knives and forks correctly or whether they slurped whilst drinking their tea from the bone china cups – for they were more used to the thick cups we normally used. Her eyes seemed always to be on me when I wanted to fidget. As I sat my thoughts were on the cakes and jelly. How I wished they'd get on, for minutes to a small boy who is bored and fed up are like hours.

Soon they finished the first course. Muriel and Harold took away the large plates. Uncle leaned back in his chair, sucking on his teeth and remarking, "That was a nice bit of ham, Robert. When did you kill the pig?"

"How could he?" I thought. He enjoyed eating the ham but in his mind he thought only of killing.

Mother then served out the jelly and cakes.

"Jelly, Gertie?"

"No, Nellie. I don't care for jelly."

"She doesn't like jelly!" I thought. "I don't want to be like her; I eat lots and lots."

The chatting seemed to get less and less as the meal came to an end. Muriel and my brothers started clearing the table. I was also allowed to carry a few things into the kitchen. I could hear those left in the dining room passing remarks about the boys, 'us'.

"When is Victor starting school? He is big for his age. How's Harold doing on the farm?" On and on they chatted.

Then they decided to have a stroll around the farm in the late evening sun. Everyone put on their Sunday hats and wandered slowly amongst the grazing cattle, stopping to admire one cow's body, her bag, how well her teats were hanging down, all too boring for me. Kicking a ball about was more exciting for me, but no – it was Sunday. Passing through the orchard as they returned to the house, Mother and Gertie were more interested in the young chicks which had hatched in the incubator a few weeks before, now beginning to lose all their fluffy down to grow proper feathers. They were not so pretty as they were when they were day-old chicks.

They wandered past my little farm of stick animals. As I tried to show Aunty my cows she turned to Mother and said, "He still plays with them. He'll make a farmer, one day."

Then taking her next step forward, she stepped on and broke a cow, which I had put out on the green grass to graze.

As we came into the yard, my father and uncle went into the stable. I wondered why they had gone in there for the horses were out in the field. Then I saw water running into the drain out of the stable door. I realised they had gone to do a 'wee-wee'.

Soon we were looking at Uncle's Rover car. To me it was big and wonderful, better than my dad's Ford, for it was long and black with a little thin gold line along the side and the headlamps were big and shiny, just like the bumpers. You stepped up onto a long running board to get in. The canvas top was stretched tight over you as you sat inside. Uncle let me sit and hold the steering wheel. It had a shiny wood rim to match the dashboard. In front was the horn, like a trumpet fixed to the side. As I sat holding the steering wheel Uncle pressed on the rubber windbag on the horn to make a sound like a horse coughing. Oh yes, it was exciting sitting there. In my mind I was doing hundreds of miles an hour, faster than my dad's Ford.

Uncle realised I did not want to get out, so he let me sit beside him as he started the car. I watched as he set the little levels in the centre of the steering wheel, then he asked

Father to crank the starting handle. Soon the engine started. I held tightly onto the dashboard. Uncle selected a gear to move off, for he was pleasing me. I could have a ride while he turned the car for his homeward journey. Then Uncle lifted me from the seat to return into the house, since by now, it was past my bedtime. Muriel and Harold had washed up all the tea things and all was tidy. You see they had to do all the tidying on such occasions on Sundays because Lizzy and Mary, the maids, did not come into work. It was their day off.

The time came when Uncle said, "Well, Robert, we shall have to be going home to see what's happened there," for they had a big farm in the neighbouring village.

Mother helped Gertie on with her coat and fur stole. "Thanks," she said.

The car started and they were soon vanishing up the lane. The last waves were made and we all returned into the house. Everyone's mood changed and an air of tension came over us, when Mother enquired if all the silver had been packed away properly and the chairs placed neatly in the dining room. She remarked on my fidgeting. But soon I was going up to bed, thinking only of sitting in Uncle's car imitating the engine noise and falling asleep with a contented smile on my face.

CHAPTER FIVE

Mondays and Tuesdays

The next thing I heard was the familiar sound of the milk buckets in the dairy and the pigs being fed. Then I realised it was another washday Monday. Everyone would be dashing about. All that milk from Sunday had to be made into cheese, which meant Muriel had no time for me, and Lizzy would be busy doing the washing. You could hear her banging the dolly peg in the wooden washtub full of clothes. From time to time Mother would come in and give her a hand, scrubbing away at the shirt collars or at any britches that were being washed that day. Steam would fill the washhouse. Everyone wore aprons made from old sacks and the clothes would be moved from tub to tub, then some would go into the blue water and the shirt collars into starch along with the white tablecloths. Mother would take the clothes from the tub whilst Lizzy had the wringer handle in the up position and the water gushed back into the tub as the clothes were passed through. Placing the clothes in the washing basket Mother and Lizzy would be seen vanishing up into the orchard and the washing would soon be seen blowing in the wind like sailing ships at sea.

Then always came the job we all hated – the kitchen. Lizzy would pile all the chairs on the table, the long bench went outside; then on her hands and knees with a scrubbing brush and a water bucket at her side, she would scrub that floor from corner to corner until you could see your face in it. Not content with just scrubbing the floor, the fire in the range was let to go low so that the flues under the oven could be cleaned, followed by blackleading until it shone. I had heard my eldest brother Bert in one of his tempers on such days saying to Mother, "You'd blacklead the bloody coal next, if you could." Those were the moments when it was best to run for cover, for a wet dishcloth or something would be flying around your ears. After the floor was scrubbed came the ritual laying of the newspapers like carpets so that the men coming in to dinner did not walk on the clean floor. This paper-laying on the floor was followed by paper laid on the long bench after it had been scrubbed outside and brought back in, so when we sat down to dinner the paper was under our bottoms.

Monday dinner, or what was known as 'washday dinner', in a farmhouse was an experience to be remembered. New cold potatoes, cold meat, gravy that was half warmed-up coming out of the pot like lumpy custard, followed by apple pie, cold with a crust as thick as a builder's plank. Topping up a lunch to be remembered was a wet bum after I'd been sitting on the cleaned bench. I was exhausted by the smell of the carbolic soap used when scrubbing the floor and, to top it all, a fire in the range that hadn't the will to burn. But mind you, one had to feed. The grate shone, the floor was scrubbed but where had my spirit gone? I felt there was more comfort sitting in the kennel with the dog.

The dishes were soon collected from the table and Lizzy would be chasing up to the orchard fetching the clothes that were dry. Then she'd put out the cheesecloths which Bert and Muriel had washed after cheese making. With the bundle of clean clothes in a basket she would put them down on the kitchen table, sorting the ones due for ironing. The larger and heavier ones were put through the mangle. Sheets would be folded to fit just the width of the wooden rollers in the mangle, then when the wheel at the end was turned the sheets were taken in between the wooden rollers. As they emerged the other side the rollers came back together again with a loud clonk. Often I would see Mother inspect the sheets to see if there were any creases left in. If there were, Lizzy would have to do them again. In the kitchen Muriel would be busy ironing away with every item folded into a neat pile. Again Mother would look at what was being done. Sometimes, if something was not done to her liking, she would take the warming iron from in front of the fire, spit on it to check if it was hot enough, then, wiping it with a cloth, she would push Muriel out of the way to do it herself. In her temper she would shout at my sister, who by then had left the kitchen.

I think everyone was glad when Monday was over.

One of the last tasks in the evening was preparing the bread dough ready for the bread-making next day. After mixing, the yeast was added and the dough was always put in a large brown earthenware bowl with a cloth over the top. Then this was placed in the long pantry to prove ready for the morning.

Tuesday started much like all the other days. After tending to the poultry outside and clearing away the breakfast dishes, Mother always attended to the bread-making. Lizzy did not come in on Tuesdays for she had to go to my Aunty Gertie's. In her place came a young lady from the village called Winnie Evans – a very happy person who did not clatter about as much as Lizzy. Her father helped on the farm at different times in the year. He was also the local gravedigger. Along with that job he also looked after the Vicar's small farm. As soon as Winnie arrived she always made sure the fire in the range was burning well, for the oven had to be hot ready for the bread-making. Then she would fetch the bowl of dough from the pantry, together with the bread tins, and place them on the table ready for Mother when she returned from her morning rounds.

I would often peep into the bowl, only to see on raising the cloth a ball of dough much bigger than I had seen the night before. Mother would come in, put on her white apron and after removing the cloth, take a knife, cut a piece of dough, put it down on the kneading board and with clenched fists start kneading away, turning and folding it about several times. After a few moments the kneaded dough would be placed in one of the baking tins. This was repeated until all the tins were used. If I was there watching, she would give me a small piece of the dough to play with. After I had rubbed it about the board she would put it in the oven along with the tins.

While this was going on in the kitchen, Winnie was busy cleaning the bedrooms, for all country households at the time had days for doing tasks about the house. Monday was washday, Tuesday was for baking, and Wednesday in our area was market day.

Soon the smell of baking bread would fill the kitchen. In fact the whole house took on the atmosphere. How Mother knew how to control the hot oven I did not know for it had no thermostats as we have today. Soon it was time to check the first batch. As the oven door was opened I could see the tops of the loaves, all brown and crisp. Mother would get close to the oven to withdraw the tins of bread from the oven shelf. She would turn the tin upside down with one hand and would tap a finger of the other hand on the bottom of the upturned tin. By the sound it made she would know if the bread was cooked or not. Sometimes it was, at other times it would be returned to the oven for a few minutes more. Then came the time when all the loaves were taken from the oven to make room for the second batch and so on.

Once out of the oven the loaves were turned out of the tins and placed on the table to cool. It was lovely to see the piping hot brown bread on the table.

Looking back and thinking about that bread, I realise that the wheat had been grown and milled here on the farm. Every bit of the grain had gone into the flour. The only added ingredients in the fifteen to twenty loaves baked, that were not produced on the farm, were the salt and yeast. No one could enjoy anything more delightful than a slice of that newly-baked bread, with home-made cheese and butter.

After the last baking, Winnie would clear away all the tins, washing and storing them ready for the next time.

Tuesday lunch was the same as Monday with one difference. The potatoes were freshly boiled.

CHAPTER SIX

Wednesdays and Thursdays

After doing the milking and feeding the animals and poultry, and as soon as breakfast was over, Bert would have to help Father get everything ready for the market on Wednesdays. There would be store pigs or calves to go; Mother would have baskets of new laid eggs, dressed and live chicks and produce from the garden according to the season. There was always a large basket of farm butter wrapped neatly in greaseproof paper. Each pound pack had the image of a cow moulded on the top.

By now, Father had started the Ford car, now converted into a truck by means of a special flat platform with side rails and a tailboard high enough to keep small animals in. The cab was a canvas cover stretched tightly over a metal frame and fastened onto the top of the windscreen. As he drove into the yard Bert would prepare to load what was being taken. The animals would be first, and then a wooden hurdle would be placed across leaving room for the other produce, which was to be placed on a thick bed of straw to avoid breaking the eggs. While Bert sheeted over the truck, Father and Mother changed into their market day clothes. Father wore a clean white shirt with a starched collar, his tie fastened with a gold pin; then his tailor-made britches, which were fastened tightly below the knee by a row of small buttons, and highly-polished leggings and boots. To this he added a hard black hat and a hooked cane. Now you had a farmer ready for market.

Mother would have a white blouse with frills down the front, a brown skirt down well below her knees, buttoned-up boots, and a straw hat held on with a large hat pin which always looked as if it had been passed right through her head from one side to the other. As she walked down the yard clutching her old handbag, her last words were always to make sure that I got on with my work, "Don't stand talking to callers." We never had callers on Wednesday for they knew where all the farmers were on market day.

You see, I was not allowed to go to market for I was too small. "Sometime, when I get older," I thought, "I would like to see what it is like." We would stand in the yard to watch them drive out of sight. As they did Muriel and Bert seemed to give a sigh of relief, for it was a strain getting everything ready as well as doing their normal routine work. I just played around.

One particular Wednesday I saw Massey the waggoner in the yard.

"Massey, what are you going to do?"

"Ah, Master Victor, I'd be going to get the mowing machine out of the cart shed."

"Can I come?"

"I don't see why not."

Soon I was walking alongside him into the cart shed where the mower had been stored all winter. As he looked down the long mower pole and started to pull I ran behind to push with all my might. Soon it was out in the yard. Then Massey started looking at every part, taking bolts out here or there, putting in new parts. As we were busying away Muriel arrived with mugs of coffee. She always made a drink when Mother was away.

"Thanks, Miss Muriel," was always Massey's reply. As she left she would enquire if I was in his way.

"Nay miss, I'll look after 'im."

As we sat on the mower drinking he said, "Well, young man, you'll be going to school after harvest they tell me. You'll be all right, then, among all the other little girls and boys."

I thought for a moment as I drank.

"Did you go to school? What is it like?"

"It's all right. But you see I went to school where they learnt thee nowt for tuppence a week. It's all right now."

Soon we were busy. He gave me the oilcan to oil the wheels. You can imagine I oiled everything including myself. I loved talking and being with Massey for he would let me blow out his match after lighting his pipe. Sometimes, he would take what looked like one of his old tobacco tins out of his pocket, and as he opened it I could see a piece or two of home-made treacle toffee. Wiping his hands down the side of his trousers he would break a piece off to give to me. Oh, it was a lovely taste.

"I like you, Massey!" would be my reply.

Soon it was dinnertime. Massey would go into the stable to have what he called his bagging. Very often it consisted of a slice of thick bread with very little butter, a thick piece of cheese, a big slice of home-made fruit cake and a drink, which would be a bottle of tea wrapped in an old sock to help to keep it warm.

While Massey was having his dinner I went into the house. Muriel, after boiling the potatoes, had mashed them up with a little butter seasoned with pepper. Also, she would often cook some bacon in the oven and nice fried egg. I liked my Wednesday dinner for it was better than cold meat. Also, there were only three of us, for Cyril and Harold were at school. None of the maids came in. Perhaps Mother wouldn't or couldn't trust them.

After dinner Muriel sat by the fire and read a story to me,

like 'Alice in Wonderland' or 'Snow White and the Seven Dwarfs', but my favourite above all others was 'Black Beauty', that poor horse. I could not understand why Muriel always asked me not to tell Mother she had been reading to me.

I was looking forward to them coming home from market for Father always brought back a few sweets. Mother would bring some fancy cakes, one for each of us. Also thin pork sausages, which she would cook in the oven until they were all brown. Wednesday was the treat of the week: pork sausages with a slice of home-cured bacon and pieces of home-made bread, which were rubbed around the plate soaking up every drop of bacon fat from around the plate. No plate needed washing after a tea like that!

As soon as the day's work was done, everybody had time to hear about market prices for the produce sold that day. Also, there might be the trying on of new hobnailed boots or clogs which Mother had bought for one of us. Sometimes it was clothes, flannelette shirts or heavy corduroy britches bought not for their fashion but for their hardwearing. As she was so very often saying, "They're a bit big, but they'll wear well." I know my brothers, who were much older than myself, were not allowed a choice of clothing, for Mother bought everything. One reason for this was that no one in the family was paid for the work they did. Father would often remind us that he could not feed and clothe us and pay wages. This way of life was common among farming people in those days.

Thursdays were days when everybody would be rushing around doing the extra jobs not done on Wednesday – cleaning boots, and turning out the bedrooms until it felt that the whole farm was being scrubbed. After breakfast, I soon got ready to go outside to see if Massey was still working with the mower. To my disappointment he had taken it into the field for mowing. Just then Father came by the shed, enquiring what I was looking for. I began to tell him about the mower.

"Oh, Massey took it to the field before you were up," he said as he walked towards the pony already harnessed to the float. He turned to me, "Jump in, I am going to see Massey." Soon Dolly was trotting up the lane at her usual speed and as always occasionally breaking wind as she went.

The field of tall grass came in sight. I could see where the mower had cut, leaving the grass lying in long swathes around the field. When we entered the field, I could see the heads of the two horses bobbing up and down over the tall grass. Soon they were turning the corner. Massey, as he sat on the sack placed over the metal seat, could be heard saying, "Woo, steady. Come back. Come on, boys." Soon I could hear the chatter of the mower's blade as it cut away at the grass. I watched, fascinated, as the grass fell into a neat swathe behind the mower. As the horses pulled on their traces their collars pressed hard onto their shoulders and as they passed by I could smell their hot bodies, the hot leather harness and the newly-mown grass. Swallows flew low over the horses' heads, collecting insects.

Father walked about the grass as it lay, and I jumped from swathe to swathe or sometimes ran in between each row of grass imagining I was a train travelling on its rails. Soon the horses were coming by again, and this time Massey stopped. Tying the plough cords to the seat of the mower, he got from his seat and pushed his cap back on his head.

"Well, Governor, it's not too bad a crop, but it is a bit thin under yon trees."

"How's the mower going, Massey?"

"Well, that young'n oiled it well yesterday," was his reply.

Then Massey bent down over the machine and pulled out the cutting blade to replace it with a newly sharpened one.

Father enquired how long he would carry on cutting, for the horses had been working since early morning. It was better working before it got hot in the summer sun. As Massey settled himself back on the mower seat he said, "Well, governor. I'll carry on 'til bagging time. Then this afternoon I'll go hoeing the turnips and let the horses have a rest."

By now Dolly had wandered over the field, eating away at the newly-mown grass. Once aboard the float we were all soon trotting back towards home. On the way we called at a nearby field to check over the young cattle grazing there. Shortly we were back in the farmyard and I returned to my stick horses lying in the orchard. Very quickly I was poking them into the ground so they stood upright and I could tie a board to them with a piece of string, which then became my mowing machine. When they were all securely tied I would walk around parts of the orchard holding on to my horses and dragging my make-believe mower behind, stopping occasionally to oil or change the cutting blades just as I had seen Massey do. It was surprising how much pleasure I got out of my stick animals and an old box or two.

Now it was time for Thursday's dinner.

I knew there would be no story time. Thursday's dinner had in it a bit of every day of the week – what I soon began to call the 'horrible pot'. For standing on the kitchen range was that brown earthenware pot which had been stewing away in the oven since early morning. Inside was a meal not unlike Aladdin's cave; everything in it. The remains of the Sunday joint cut into one-inch cubes (some of them all fat, some lean meat), the bones of the joint, potatoes sliced or not, carrots and parsnips (some of which were sliced like long fingers) all flavoured by only one vegetable – the big onion. As we all sat around the table, this brown pot would be placed in front of Mother. Then with a big ladle in hand she would serve platefuls of this steaming hot 'culinary delight'. Sometimes I would be lucky and get chunks of lean meat; more often than not I had a share of fat. The vegetables were not too bad as long as you had plenty of gravy. No matter how many pieces of dry bread I had with it, I hated those 'hot pot' dinners and to this very day I cannot bring myself to enjoy chopped-up meat and vegetables cooked in this way.

Following would be the remains of cold pies; odd pieces of apple, plum or gooseberry. The pastry by this day was hard on top but soggy at the bottom. A dinner like that was called good and wholesome in the 1920s but it was certainly not fancy.

By now I had to get the coal and sticks in for lighting the fire each day. It was a big bore, for I wanted to play around the farm with the dogs. Should I forget, Mother would search me out, forcefully reminding me about those damned sticks and coal. I would go into the coal shed crying and sucking my thumb. Very often Rover would come in with me. I sat wishing I was a big man so that I didn't have to get sticks in. Rover was very often beside me, looking up into my face as if he knew how I felt. He'd tap his paw on my leg as if to give me a most needed word of comfort. After a while I would emerge with the coal in a bucket and sticks under one arm, hands black, except for the thumb I had been sucking. Dust had settled on my face where tears had rolled. I would struggle around the house. When I put down my load by the boiler Mother in her cold voice would say, "You haven't filled that bucket. Go and get some more." No one seemed to understand I didn't want to get coal, but it had to be.

One Thursday afternoon, a neighbour called Jack Wittingham came into the yard to see Father about borrowing our seed drill. While Mother was making the usual enquiries about his parents and generally passing the time of day Father came into the yard, asking, "Hello Jack, what are you after today?"

"It's like this, boss. We want to sow a couple of acres of kale and we thought like you wouldn't mind giving us a lend of your seed drill. That's if you are not using it."

"I thought that you wanted something to come and see us this time of day, for I thought you would be milking."

"You see," said Jack, smiling as he spoke, "I always leaves the work to those who want to do it."

At long last Jack got what he wanted, the loan of the seed drill.

"I'll send someone with the horse tomorrow."

As he turned to leave he pulled his hand out of his pocket and gave me a sixpence.

"Here, take that. Put that in your money box and wash your face before I come again."

By the yard gate he had left his cycle. After lighting a cigarette this tall figure of a man rode away up the lane. He didn't press on the pedals with his soles of his feet – like most people do – but with his heels, the toes of his big boots pointing out sideways.

This was the time of the afternoon when the cows were coming into the yard and sheds for the milking. Massey could be seen walking down the lane. Muriel was in the cow house. Harold and Cyril had changed from their school clothes. Everybody had put on their milking jackets, then on collecting their three-legged milking stools and a bucket they started milking.

Massey had a stool with one centre leg; attached to it was a leather strap by which he tied the stool to himself so when he sat down the stool was already underneath him. There he sat, with the milk bucket between his knees, balanced on his one-legged stool. As he moved from cow to cow I could see the stool sticking out behind him from under the milking jacket. As the buckets became full of fresh warm milk, Bert carried them across the yard into the dairy, emptying the milk into the cheese vats ready for the following day's cheese making. When milking time was coming to an end, I remember seeing some eight or nine cats waiting by their milk dish, which was always placed by the last cows to be milked. It was as if the cats knew the time. When the milk was poured into their dish they all soon started lapping it up.

In between carrying milk to the dairy, Bert had prepared the calf feeding buckets into which a ration of milk was poured for each calf. Each was given a different amount of milk according to its age. As the milking came to an end, the cows returned to the field. I watched Massey going home. As he was walking up the lane he had his coat over one shoulder, his can of milk down by his side and, drifting over his shoulders behind him, the smoke from his pipe.

CHAPTER SEVEN

Schooldays

School! Yes, the day has come that everybody has been telling me stories about. For example, how Mr Wood the headmaster gave naughty boys and girls the cane, and how you had to sit still, and do writing, reading and sums. The infants class was taught by a lady, Miss Elizabeth Taylor, who lived in a neighbouring village. I had met her many times before when she called at home as a friend of my mother's, collecting for some village function or other.

When I got out of my warm bed, I looked out of the window to see rain and no sun. It was September, three days before my fourth birthday. Mother came in the bedroom, to wash and dress me up in my Sunday best clothes.

No one else knows how I felt at that time, but it is still etched on my memory. I had never been away from the farm other than on market days with my parents, with Muriel on her bicycle to visit Grandma and friends, to a few birthday parties of cousins, and to neighbouring farm parties. What would happen to my friend Rover and all the other animals? This was my world falling apart.

Breakfast that morning was a labour of need, not because I wanted it. All I could think of was Mr Wood's cane and boys fighting in the playground. Where would I go to wee or get a drink? My thoughts were like this morning, foggy and wet. Nobody was saying the right things to me. Oh dear, where was I going?

The moment came when my brother Harold, nine years older with only a few more months at school, said, "Overcoats on, let's go."

He had brought a clean corn sack in to put over our shoulder because of the rain. With me on his back, off we set for the mile walk across the fields to school. As we got over the hedge into the road leading down to the school he took off the wet sack and left it under the hedge, to be collected on the way home.

Soon we were going up the steps into the schoolyard with all the other boys and girls around. How I felt is difficult for me to recall; I was a frightened child who had never known or experienced the world away from home, without my parents. All I knew was cows, pigs, horses and hens together with all that went on around the farm. In fact as the old countryman said, "You've still got straw in ye' ears and muck on ye' boots." Adding to all this, I was thinking of the stories I had been told about the headmaster and how he would cane me if I misbehaved. It was like entering a new world.

Soon the bell rang out. All the boys and girls stood in straight lines facing the entrance door. I stood by my brother Harold. You could have heard a pin drop. Then next I saw was Mr Wood the Head standing in the doorway complete with cane.

"Good morning, children," he said.

"Good morning, Sir," came the reply as we filed into school.

Mr Wood stood aside looking down at our shoes and socks. We were pulled up if he was not satisfied. The children not up to standard had to stand in front of class while he rebuked them.

After Morning Prayer, I sat down with my brother.

The classroom was something I never had experienced

Hinstock School, with its high windows, from a postcard published by District View Publishing Company, 117 Loughborough Rd, Leicester.

The Falcon, Hinstock, from a postcard published by District View Publishing Company, 117 Loughborough Rd, Leicester.

Hinstock church, from a postcard published by District View Publishing Company, 117 Loughborough Rd, Leicester.

A black and white cottage in Hinstock, from a postcard published by District View Publishing Company, 117 Loughborough Rd, Leicester.

before. It was large, high and had a fireplace at one end where Mr Wood stood at his desk. The walls at the side were covered with dark brown tiles up to the bottom of the windows, some five feet from the floor. Although the windows were large, with nine-inch square panels, one could not see a thing of the outside.

The desks were long and dark brown, set out in rows seating six pupils, with inkpots fitted along the front.

As I sat by my brother I felt so sad and frightened, wishing I could go home and be with the animals.

It was not long before Miss Taylor, the infants teacher, came to collect me. As she held my hand to take me to her classroom, leaving Harold behind, I felt worried and sad. But she had what you would call warmth and a caring love in her voice as she walked through the school with me. I then became more relaxed. What helped also was that I had met her before.

Arriving in the room just like the other, with brown tiles and high windows you could not see through, she asked me where I would like to sit, saying, "You would like to be with Elizabeth – you know her, for I believe you have gone to her birthday parties."

Yes, Elizabeth was another farmer's daughter and family friend. Also, I found out that I was not the only new boy. That soon made me feel relaxed and the sadness went.

The register completed, the teacher told us to fold our arms and place them on the desk for she was going to read a story to us. 'Little Red Riding Hood' – I still remember it to this day, and how her voice and expression made it so easy to listen to. In fact, it took away all my fears. Also, I was sharing with my sweetheart.

Story over, we had to get our slates and chalk to draw figures of Little Red Riding Hood or the Wolf and house. While doing this Elizabeth's chalk fell on the floor. When she got up from picking it up, she said at the top of her voice, "Miss, Victor has wet on the floor." The others in the class smiled. Miss came over, and seeing the state I was in took me over to a large cupboard in the corner of the room. Opening the doors you could see items of clothing for all occasions. Soon I was clean and dry again. The teacher told me to put my hand up and ask to leave the room next time.

Then it was playtime, when I made a friend. John Williamson was also a farmer's son, his grandfather was our vet and a great friend of my father. So, you see, things were beginning to fall into place.

Eventually I ventured into the toilets: what an experience! A long dark shed with a partly covered corrugated tin roof. The long wall was painted with black tar, and underneath was an equally long open gully. Boys with trouser legs pulled up were peeing onto the wall. What a sight! "Give me a tree or haystack at home," I thought.

Back in the classroom we were forming the letters, A, B, C, etc. I liked that, for the teacher told us to draw images such as 'A' for apple, 'B' for bee, 'W' for wasp. Draw that. That way of teaching helped me and the other children to spell and draw; being country children added meanings to the symbols.

Lunchtime soon came and I joined Harold, for he had the tuck box with a bottle of home-made lemonade. The girls played hopscotch, the boys played football. As the playground was much higher than the main Liverpool Road, I could look over a wall down onto the road. I loved watching the Sentinel Steam Wagons pulling up the hill, sparks flying from their funnels. Oh, the smell of hot steam and coal! These wagons were mostly carrying stone and rock for road making.

The week passed so quickly. I had my fourth birthday when I was made to stand in front of class while they sang

"Happy Birthday" to me. In fact, by this time I was enjoying school, making many new friends. The worry and fear had all but gone and I had lots to tell my sister Muriel and all at home. But I missed the animals very much.

The days and weeks just melted away, with me enjoying all the lessons we did, making more friends, and always experiencing more things to learn and do. For instance, one morning the local nurse called in school to check our hair for fleas, and also inspect our general body condition. We called her the 'bug-hunter'. Also, the school doctor had called to examine us all. This was carried out at the top of the room which had been sheeted off. Some of the children had doctor's notes for their parents.

Next was the school dentist. It was all clear for me.

With all this and normal classwork going on, Christmas soon arrived, and three weeks' holiday.

My life during the holiday was just the same as before, with the cows being fed and cheese and butter being made. In fact, all the animals had to be attended; only the horses had a rest.

On Christmas Day and Boxing Day we had visitors including my uncle and aunt, bringing presents of knitted woollen stockings for school and lots of sweets. Mother had bought me a new school cap, and a pair of clogs with wooden soles for when the snow came, saying, "They'll keep your feet dry, going to school." All the presents had a practical role, including my first school bag.

The best evening was when Jeff Farr, a neighbour, came with his magic lantern to show us his new glass slides of African animals. The paraffin lamp lit, the white bed sheet hung down over the kitchen cupboard, he would slide the glass strips through the projector lens and then images of lions, tigers and elephants would be seen on the sheet. At times, as he pushed the slide through, he would move the slide back and forth giving the impression the animals were running. For me this was the best evening of the holiday.

The festive time of eating turkey, plum pudding, dates, figs and dishes of nuts came to an end, and talk came back to work and school.

The morning I was waiting for arrived. I had lost my initial fear of Mr Wood and his cane, for he had been most helpful to me. Also I was looking forward to seeing what presents my friends had received for Christmas.

A young boy dressed for school, I now wore a new cap, a new flannelette shirt, a tie that was white with black bars, new corduroy trousers (a little on the big side, Mother's idea being that "you'll grow into them") that rubbed my inside leg sore as I walked, and long stockings complete with tight elastic bands just below the knee.

I put my overcoat on, with my gloves attached to the sleeves with a short piece of tape. My shoes were all bright and shiny. There was no snow, so no clogs were necessary, and I went away to school like a young country gentleman.

At school, I had to go through infants' gate, for I was not to go with my brothers Harold and Cyril into the seniors' area. I had my own tuck box in my new school bag. It was wonderful meeting my little pals and listening to the teacher's stories, 'Alice in Wonderland', 'Robinson Crusoe', and many others. Sums and writing I enjoyed.

One day a month the vicar would come and talk to us about Christ, the church and religion. Then he would invite questions. This I liked very much.

The following days and weeks seemed to be similar but at the same time we were learning, seeing new things. On occasions Miss Taylor would read a story. Then we would enact the characters, dressing up in clothes that she brought out of that long cupboard in the classroom. I loved playing the part of the Woodman and many others.

The cold Winter weather was giving way to the Spring sunshine. Our activities changed, for we spent time outside in the playground with the teacher instructing us in team games, P.T. and body deportment. She made us aware that "one has to live and understand other people." As she used to say, "You are but a small spoke in the wheel of the world."

Back in school, we started writing joined-up letters together to form simple words i.e. 'pig', 'horse', 'elephant', 'yes' and 'no'. Later in the day we did sums, putting numbers in line, i.e. 1+3+2=6, in many forms. Time seemed to fly by until going-home time. Now I did not have to wait for my brother, but with my friend John and others we used to run down his grandpa's field until I could get over the fence into father's field. When it was Springtime, more often than not, I was going through the newborn lambs and their mothers, trying to count them as I went, though I found that was an impossible task. If I saw one that was not well I told someone at home.

When I told Father about the difficulty I had counting sheep, he replied jokingly, "It's like this, son, you count their feet and then divide by four – easy!"

CHAPTER EIGHT

Summer on the farm

$\mathcal{I}$ realised by now that school and work around the farm repeated themselves season after season. Learning in school was developing my mind and body. Things on the farm were not so important for me as they had been before I went to school. The first three years at school passed so quickly, and people changed. My brother Harold had left and I did not rely on Cyril. I was developing my own views of life – in other words, growing up.

The summer sun was getting warmer, and the days were much lighter for longer. Also, this was my last term in the infants with Miss Taylor. After the summer holidays I would be with my friend going up into the seniors' section – something none of us was looking forward to.

When the holidays came, haymaking was in full swing. Soon I was leading the horse backwards and forwards from the field, bringing the hay to the stack yard to be unloaded. Then I returned to the field very tired. The large shod feet of the Shire horse used to catch the back of my ankle and heel, making them sore and bleed. The reason for this was that my short arms did not allow enough distance between the horse and me.

Once my shoelace came undone so I loosed hold of the bridle and bent down to tie it, just getting up as the large cartwheel touched the bottom of my back. Years later, thinking about this, I realised that big cartwheel could have gone

72

over me, perhaps killing me. I should have stopped the horse before I bent down. I never told my parents. Really I was too young to be in charge of such powerful animals, and it was unsafe. When I went into the house in the late evening, tired and weary, I showed my mother my bloody heels. All she would say was: "Get them washed. They'll be better in the morning."

One day Mother had filled a big basket with sandwiches and a large jar of cider, and told me to take it out to those who were working on in the hay field. It was a very hot day. What did I do? I started taking a little taste of the cider, taking larger tastes as I went. By the time I arrived in the field, my legs were very weak. My brother Harold asked, "Has the sun got to you?" Before I answered Massey said, "The young bugger has been at the bloody cider." For days after they would ask, "How's your head?"

The large brown earthenware cider jar had a narrow neck and cork, and handles to lift it by. Its capacity was just over the half gallon when it was full, and it took two hands to lift it. My deeds for that day were talked about for days. I do not think that Father was impressed.

With the harvest in full swing, I also had to milk a few quiet cows and then feed the calves. I did not mind this for it gave me a chance to have a sit down. When you are six or seven, you get a little tired. My time from school was filled with more and more jobs around the farm.

In the summer evenings I enjoyed sitting outside with Father and Mr Cork. The front of the farmhouse faced south and in the far distance we could see the small Shropshire mountain, The Wrekin. To the right the warm evening sun would be setting and immediately in front of us was the neatly-cut tennis court, bounded by a hedge and fruiting damson trees, a border of beautiful coloured roses, the kitchen gardens, and a field beyond with the cows peacefully grazing. I loved the evening song of the skylark high in the sky, followed by the wonderful high-pitched continuous note as he dropped down to earth. Adding to all this we could hear a pheasant calling friends before he flew up to roost in his favourite tree. We might even hear the fox bark out as he started his nightly rounds.

One night, Father and Mr Cork chatted about cows and the harvest, and Mr Cork talked about three fat bacon pigs which he would be sending to market in midweek.

There was a moment of silence, and suddenly Mr Cork said, "You know Boss, it's great sitting here. I've just been a-thinking. You know Boss, there's more going on in those hedgerows than in London, for there's a-killing, there's a-dying, a-lovemaking and a-singing. There's a-worrying. Ah, if only we could see it. Soon it will all go quiet as, like us, they'll be going to sleep, then there's be a-robbings. Thanks for the cider and Missus' fruitcake; I'll be on my way."

On went his old bowler and he walked off, his big feet anchoring his bowed legs. Soon the call came for my bedtime but I had to imitate Mr Cork as I went.

Next morning the day started like other days. Milking, cheese-making, and so on. Father had checked the animals informing us that he had put a cow into a loose box, telling me to keep an eye on her, saying that if she started calving I was to fetch him from the stack yard. So I went about my jobs. I peeped over the door mid-morning. I could see two little feet out of the back of her, so off I went to the stack yard for Father. Soon he was on his way, followed by Mr Owen and Bert, who had a rope at hand. Father, after washing his hands and arms in soapy water, washed around the cow's tail. He examined inside the cow to see if everything was right for the calf to come into the world. Tying the rope to the calf's feet, he told the others to pull. It was then I realised I was seeing my first birthing of a calf. I remember the noise to this day. Soon the calf was lying in the straw and Father was washing its nose out. The cow got up, looked at her baby and started licking it. All was well.

The calf was now up on its legs. Its mother had licked it all clean, showing a beautiful red colour with white legs from the knees down and a small white marking on its forehead. Soon, like all newborn animals, it was searching for its mother's teats and milk – to this day I do not know what gives baby animals this instinct. Watching little pigs being born is just wonderful again. As soon as a piglet's legs bear its weight it starts searching for teats and milk. We used to call the rows of teats on a sow's stomach 'The Milk Bar'.

The hay harvest was slowing down and the stacks got bigger and shaped ready for thatching. We then turned to other seasonal jobs for in two days' time the vet was coming to castrate the lambs and cut off their tails.

The day came; my brother Harold had penned the sheep up; the ewes in one pen, the lambs in another. Oh, the noise of the lambs calling for their mothers made me feel like putting them together again! Everything was ready, i.e. the fire bucket glowing hot with docking irons getting red and the wooden block in position. The docking iron had a long handle on one end a wooden handle grip; the other end, a spade-like blade which was made red hot repeatedly. For the lamb's tails were pulled straight over the wooden block, then this hot blade was forced through the tail cutting away the unwanted part and at the same time sealing the veins to

Docking Iron

stop the bleeding. After this all the male lambs were cas-
trated. Then after the wool on every one had been checked
for fly grubs and their feet had been inspected for foot rot,
they were returned to the field and each ewe was reunited
with her lambs.

At the appropriate moment male piglets were also cas-
trated, supposedly to produce better tasting bacon and pork
joints.

The following morning following the lambs' ordeal I went
with my brother to check the sheep, taking them their daily
ration of corn and hay. To my joy and surprise the lambs
were skipping about as they suckled off their mothers and
wagged their little stumpy tails as if nothing had happened.
They all seemed well and hearty.

The next thing to do with the ewes was the dipping in disinfectant to protect them from flies laying eggs in their woolly coats, for if they were not removed they hatched out into
small grubs that ate into the sheep's flesh.

When I got to the house I got all the small jobs completed
quickly, for in the afternoon a school friend was coming to
see me. When he arrived I had lots to show and tell him
about the newborn calf and had to tell him what had been
done to the lambs. Soon we were going to the fields looking
for birds' nests and to our surprise we saw a Pie-Wit (Plover)
running through the grass followed by her little grey
coloured chicks. It was wonderful to see. The cock bird was
flying and diving making a horrible screaming noise at
times almost touching our heads with its wings, to protect
the growing chicks and to drive us away. As we looked into
the hedges it was not long before we found a blackbird's
nest. In it was three eggs. We were careful not to damage the
nest or eggs in any way for we thought of how the bird had
collected different dried grasses. The longer hard grass on
the outside formed the shape and size of the nest and then

shorter softer grass was used for lining the inside. The final lining was always the softer grass with a few pieces of moss woven in. In comparison with some other birds, a blackbird's nest is simple and practical in construction. A thrush's nest is similar but lined inside with a covering of mud, which the bird has smoothed round; so smooth a plasterer would be proud of it. One could go on describing birds' nests and their locations for a long, long while. As we sat in the field we asked one another "How do birds know how to build?" for we had to be taught to do things such as read and write. It is easy to say that it is a natural instinct that we all have, man or beast, but it is a difficult question.

We went back to the farm to have a game of hide and seek around the haystacks and empty carts. Soon Muriel's voice was heard calling us for tea. We soon got on our way, for she put a tray full of food on the lawn for us.

Soon we were pulling off the white cloth to reveal a plate of home-cured ham sandwiches, home-made buttered tea-cakes, pieces of fresh lettuce from the garden along with other salad and fruit. We young lads soon ate it all. The buttered teacakes were followed by slices of farmhouse fruit-cake, which I had seen being baked two days previously; now, the afters – just what two young boys like – jelly and custard.

Appetites replete, we swilled it all down with some home-made lemonade.

Then we found tennis rackets to have a knockabout on the tennis court. But alas, all good things come to an end, for it was time for John to go. Across the field I went with him to our boundary fence, closely followed by Rover. We said our "goodbyes" and John went home.

Walking back to the house I could only think what a good day we had, also of all the birds' nests we had seen. When I went to bed that night I asked Muriel as she tucked me in,

"Who made the first birds and told them how to make their nests?"

All she could say was that Jesus made all creatures great and small. I went to sleep wondering who had told him how to do it.

CHAPTER NINE

Peck Mill

The next morning while I was dressing I could only think of the wonderful day we'd had the day before and the tea we'd had on the lawn. Conversation at breakfast was not about cows and milk but the preparation of cheese for a forthcoming show – for the best farmhouse cheese and butter of all England – to be held in Nantwich, South Cheshire, the recognised centre for dairy produce.

Also, as the hay harvest was all but completed and the grain harvest was not ready, Father told us that he and Mother would go and see his sister, my Aunt Cissy. She farmed at Peck Mill near Frodsham in mid-Cheshire on what used to be my father's home farm. He was going to take me with them. By this time Father had sold the old Ford car and bought a Morris saloon to which he had fitted a tow bar. He had also bought a trailer to carry all the farm produce to market on Wednesdays. There was no more packing it inside the vehicle.

The day we were going on our journey was a Tuesday. With bags all packed, off we went. I felt excited and great sitting in a car with leather seats and no draughts. Also, father did not have to stop at the canalside to top up the radiator with water. Mother had made sandwiches and cakes to eat. We stopped for a rest, a meal and a 'tiddle' near a wooded area. Then, on we went.

The journey seemed so long and tiring and I fell asleep,

only to be awakened at Peck Mill by Aunt Cissy's two daughters, Molly and Elsie, and a little white dog called Snowy. While Father was being welcomed, Molly took hold of my hand. As I entered the house via the back kitchen I saw some familiar items: a butter churn in one corner, buckets of food for some of the animals and eggs waiting to be washed. It was just like home but without the cheese presses. Along one wall was a large cooking range with shiny oven handles and hinges, complete with a lovely hot fire glowing.

Then we went into a dining and sitting room. This, too, had a big fireplace with a log burning brightly. I could not take my eyes off a polished brass pan with a long wooden handle hanging at one end of the fireplace. On the other side hung brass fire-irons. On the hearth in front of the fire was a large brass fender. They were all polished so brightly that I could see my face in them.

On the floor was a large sheepskin hearthrug on which the little dog settled. I was fascinated by the great oak beams supporting the low ceilings and the polished horse brasses of all shapes and sizes. On the shelves around the room were more brass jugs with many cut-glass vases and jugs. On the mantelshelf were models of farm animals. The furniture was made of dark oak, polished like the brass, reflecting all around the room. As I sat on the couch under the window I gazed at all the new things around me. At home, our rooms were much higher and brighter, and Mother did not like to have the brass pieces displayed like that.

After a big meal of roast beef, potatoes and carrots, followed by a lovely treacle pudding and custard, I played with the dog and a ball – which he enjoyed.

Mother took me up to the bedroom. Again this had a very low ceiling. In one corner of the large room a very small bed had been made up for me. Next to that was a large bed for my parents. While she was undressing me I asked what they did with the pan hanging by the fire downstairs. "That's a bed warming pan," she explained. "On cold winter nights people used to put hot cinders from the fire into it, then push it down the bed to warm the bedclothes, moving it all the while so not to burn the sheets."

Next morning I woke quite early and soon Molly brought in a cup of tea for my mum and dad. Then taking hold of my clothes she took me downstairs to the kitchen to wash and dress, using a large bowl of hot water. They had no bathroom. Soon I was dressed and she took me out to see the swans on the millpond*. Then we went into the cow house to meet her brother James who was milking the few cows they had. He lived in a cottage up the lane. He also had two boys of a similar age to me.

Again, the buildings were low and dark inside. Returning to the house for breakfast, we entered the kitchen. I was greeted by the smell of cooking bacon, the steam from the iron porridge saucepan and the aroma of coffee being prepared on that great black range. Attending to it all was Joan, wearing a long ankle-length dress and a white apron, with a matching frilly bonnet on her head. While this was going on, Snowy the dog was sitting waiting for any titbits falling his way.

Aunt Cissy was in the dining room preparing the table with knives, forks and coffee cups – all that was required for breakfast.

*Peck Mill lies on the edge of Alvanley, south of Frodsham and Helsby, and east of Dunham on the Hill. Sadly, in the 1965 survey of Cheshire watermills it was described as "derelict". The millpond took its water from Peck Mill Brook; this stream went on to supply Helsby Mill and is known along this part of its course as Hornsmill Brook. Where it goes into the Mersey estuary it is called the Hoolpool Gutter. According to the North West Mills Group of the Society for the Preservation of Ancient Buildings, Peck Mill may have been on a medieval site and was certainly in existence in the 18th century. The farmhouse is still there and the field shapes are virtually the same as in Victor's day but the millpond has been filled in.

Soon we were all seated around the table. Cissy gave a little cough, asking Father to read a short morning prayer which she had marked in the small Bible she had placed before him.

This over, porridge arrived followed by that wonderful home-cured bacon. Coffee was served to all the others but I was given cold milk, which I hated.

After breakfast I was taken to look around. We looked at the half-thatched house and the big uneven roof tiles which were not only on the rest of the house but on the farm buildings too. The house and buildings were made of rough sandstone blocks. I did not like this at all for it all looked low and dirty, not like the bright and clean brickwork at home. As we walked across the yard towards the mill, I asked Father why it was all built this way and where all the stone came from. He replied that many, many years before he was born the sandstone would have been dug from the millpond when they built it and the mill. He also explained in simple terms that the joints between the stone blocks were of clay also dug from the pond and that men would have sat in this very yard shaping the stone into the blocks with what they called ironstone hacks.

Soon we entered the mill. This again was roughly built with big beams cut from tree trunks. It seemed to be full of ropes and wooden wheels used as gears. We all went through to the back of the millhouse where I saw a great big iron-spoked wheel – half of it down in the stone-built channel. I felt a little frightened, so I held onto Father's hand tightly, for in the bottom of this channel one could hear water rushing down the millstream. When we got closer to the wheel we saw two men repairing the wooden 'troughs' which were bolted to the wheel, replacing the ones which were damaged or rotten. Soon I realised that James was standing inside the wheel tightening up bolts and attending to bearings on the large axle shaft. As I stood there Father explained to me how the great wheel worked.

"You see that is what they call a floodgate. A tall wooden structure incorporating a wooden door slide which is raised to allow water to rush over the wheel, filling the troughs on one side. The weight of water makes the wheel turn. As the troughs get to the bottom of the deep channel they empty into the millstream. As the wheel turns, the troughs at the top fill up again and as long as the flood gate is open the process continues."

Then he took me back into the mill, taking me up ladders to the top floor and there, looking through a slot in the wall, I could see the size of the millpond. It looked like a big lake to me. On this floor was a large wooden hopper into which the sacks of grain were tipped. Bolted to the beam overhead was a drum-like construction with a thick rope around it. The rope had a bead near the end and on the very end was a metal ring. Father explained how it all worked from the shaft that came up through the floor from the mill-wheel. A man on the ground floor would pull on the smaller rope that I could see to allow a lead ball to take the larger rope through the hole in the floor down to the ground floor. Then the miller would tie on a sack of grain and on pulling on the small rope again the drum would turn pulling up the sack through the trap doors in the floors below. I cannot remember if Father said that they pulled on the small rope whilst the sack was raised.

The grain was emptied into the bin and directed to the different floors, via wooden tubes and shutters, according to the standard of grind that was required. The small stones were on the top floor. When we came back to the ground floor I saw a great stone about twice my height leaning against the wall. Father said it was waiting to be 'dressed'. Seeing I did not understand, he explained that this meant re-cutting the grooves in the stone face, for if they were not of the right depth they would not grind the grain to flour properly.

The whole building seemed full of ropes, home-made wooden tubes and wooden gears. I asked why all the gears and moving cogs were not made of iron as they were at home, and my father replied that if they had iron gears, and these made a spark, the milling flour could catch fire. Wooden gears were safer.

As we walked back to the house for lunch he told me never to go into the mill on my own when it was working.

When lunch was over, James came in to tell us they had completed the repairs on the mill-wheel and that he would be starting it shortly. Father finished his drink and took me back to the mill. The big sacks of wheat were waiting on the ground floor. Father took me to the back door so that I would see the floodgate opened. The man waiting shouted back that he was lifting now. I stood to watch, frightened and holding on to Father very tightly. Soon water began to flow down the chute, filling the troughs on one side of the wheel. The weight of the water soon made the wheel turn. The more water he let down the chute, the faster the wheel turned.

Father then took me back into the mill where I saw the shaft from outside begin to turn the vertical shaft that went to the top of the mill. Soon I saw the rope with the lead ball come through the hole from the floor above. James looped the end of the rope with the ring around the neck of the sack, shouting to the man on the top floor, "Here it comes!" When James pulled on the thinner rope the sack lifted off the floor, and as it went it lifted the big trap doors in the floor above. As the sack cleared the doors they came down again with a big bang which frightened me still more. Father stood back by the open door and I could see the big grindstone turning and flour beginning to come down the chute into the waiting sack. By now I was getting used to all the noise. As we went back to the house, Father tried to explain how all the different stones worked but it was difficult for a young boy like me to understand.

The following morning he said he would take Mother and his sister to Liverpool so they could go shopping and he could take them around the town. Breakfast over, off we set and soon arrived in Liverpool. After parking and arranging a time and place for lunch, we went our separate ways.

The first thing I saw was the overhead railway high above the street. Next Father took me to the docks to see the large ships unloading cargo onto the rail trucks drawn by a small steam engine, and also onto horse-drawn wagons. Strongest of all these were the dockers, pushing their wheelbarrows laden with boxes. The ships were enormous, with thick ropes holding them to the quayside. I felt it was a little too much to comprehend.

After lunch we were soon on our way back to Peck Mill. Tiredness overcame me and I fell asleep on the back seat of the car.

That night when I went to bed I could not go to sleep for thinking about watching the mill working for the first time and going to the city: it was all so overwhelming for a farmer's boy.

Next morning I was tired and did not want to get up for I had been dreaming about what I had seen in Liverpool. Mother washed and dressed me, then we went down to breakfast which followed the same daily routine.

Afterwards, Auntie Cissy asked Father if he would look over the farm accounts and other family matters with her. She said I could go and play around in the yard with the dog. Their warning words as they went towards the front room were "Don't go near the mill."

The morning passed with me playing ball with the dog

and seeing the farmers coming to bring grain for milling, then taking the already milled grain away in their horse and carts.

Molly called me for lunch and while I was washing my hands said she would take me into the orchard to collect Victoria plums.

During lunch mother was talking about leaving tomorrow and saying how she had enjoyed the rest. As a young boy, I hadn't found it at all relaxing, for everyone around was older and I felt I did not fit in.

In the middle of the afternoon Molly took me over a bridge made up of two wobbly planks and a shaky hand rail which spanned the millstream, now running very fast from the mill-wheel. As we got into the orchard I saw pear, apple and plum trees; gooseberry, blackcurrant and redcurrant bushes; in fact, fruits of all kinds. While we gathered Victoria plums, which were red and as big as my fist, all juicy, I ate one, then another, until Molly told me to stop.

"Just one more, or you will get tummy ache," she said. That night when I went to bed, you know what I had – a bad tummy ache, so much so that I had to run over to the commode in the bedroom. Mother was not that pleased with me, telling me off for eating too many plums, for we were travelling home the next day.

The following morning, breakfast over, the car packed and all goodbyes said, off we set for home.

On the way Father stopped at a café near to Nantwich. As we entered a lady came over to take us to a table. She pulled the chairs out for Mother, Father and myself. Seeing I was still positioned too low to reach the table, she went and got a cushion for me to sit on. Then another lady came for our order. I could not take my eyes off her, for she was wearing a long black dress. Over it she had a beautiful white pleated apron tied at the back with a big white bow, and on her head a matching white bonnet.

She asked what 'Sir' and 'Madam' would care for; Father ordered a pot of tea and a few sandwiches, a plate of cakes and lemonade. It all duly came to the table with a lovely china tea service. The teapot was covered with blue flowers, and my drink was in a thin glass. When lunch was over, my father paid. As we walked towards the door, the lady in black whom we'd met first came over and opened it, saying "Good day, Sir, Madam and young Master. Do call again".

On our way, we soon came to farms and people Father knew, so he passed remarks about how well their crops looked – or not. I slept during the journey, only to wake up as we turned into the yard, where we were greeted by Rover wagging his tail. He was so pleased to see us back. I was pleased to see him!

Muriel came out to meet us and Mother told her all the news. Father asked Bert how things had gone while he was away. "All right," was the reply. As for myself, I just fell back into the old routine, from time to time telling my brothers about the mill-wheel being repaired and how it worked, also what I'd seen in Liverpool – and how the big ships, and the men rushing about with barrows, had frightened me a bit.

At teatime the conversation got back to its usual boring topics of cows, milk, cheese-making and hens. There was one important piece of news that Harold had to tell father – Jack Whittingham's father had died. They had asked if Massey could lead the horse at the funeral, for they were using the dray to carry the coffin to the church on Tuesday. Father agreed to what Harold had arranged.

Next morning, looking around the farm, I saw Massey had got the binder out and was ready for cutting wheat. Two of them had scythed away around the wheat field to allow the horse and binder to go around the field without knocking the growing grain down. Everything was ready for a fine day.

On Monday morning Bert came in the house after fetching the cows for early milking. At the top of his voice he shouted, "Mother, you shut the hens up in the field."

"Why?" came the reply.

"You'd had better go around and look."

Hearing all the noise I quickly got dressed to go with Mother. When we came close to the fowl pen we saw dead hens lying all around. Most of them had their heads bitten off and a few were partly eaten. Mother said there were twenty-five hens killed and many more had feathers missing. The fox had paid a visit to the unlocked fowl house. It was Mother's job to go around shutting the fowl up – if it had been someone else's their head would have rolled.

The talking points for the rest of the day were the fox's visit and Mr Whittingham's funeral.

Father had his lunch early on Tuesday, so he could get dressed for the funeral. When he came downstairs dressed in a black suit with a white shirt and black tie, Mary gave him his polished black shoes. He looked every bit like a country gentleman. As he left the house I asked him if I could come up the lane with him.

"Yes, but stand back when they come down the road to the corner."

We stood there waiting. Soon we saw the dray and Massey leading the horse. As it turned toward the church I saw Massey dressed in black with a bowler hat on. The horse's harness was all cleaned and oiled. The dray carrying the coffin was decorated with flowers. The pony and trap in which Jack and his mother sat was similarly decorated. Even the horses seemed to bow their heads. On they went. Father joined the followers for the mile walk to church. It was like a picture out of a storybook.

I turned for home thinking of men dressed in a way that I

had never seen. The white hair on horse's legs had been washed snow-white, not like when I saw them ploughing the fields.

As I went down the lane I saw Rover coming to meet me. He, too, was very quiet – just as if he knew something was different.

When I went to bed that night I realised it was the last week of my summer holidays. What a holiday! I had helped with the hay harvest and very nearly got drunk on cider; seen my first calf born; been to Peck Mill; seen the big water wheel repaired and the mill working; been to Liverpool to the ships in the docks and also seen the overhead railway. Now today I'd seen my first funeral. Before I went to sleep I hoped I should see the wheat being cut. I prayed "Please Lord, send some sunny days."

CHAPTER TEN

The last days of Summer

ednesday, next morning, the sun was shining and there was a drying light wind. I heard Father say to Massey that if it was like this at 11 o'clock he should start cutting the wheat.

The time came. I saw the horses being harnessed up to the binder, soon to go to the field. I followed on behind into the field. Massey and Cyril had to change two poles by which the horse pulled the binder to a different position at the side of the machine. They bolted on the sails arm which pushed the grain down onto the binder's moving bed. Then a set of canvas belts took the grain into the machine. All parts went around a big wheel inside the machine. Added to this, a chain similar to a cycle chain was attached, and as the horses pulled the wheel it went round, making all working parts do their job.

While the preparation was going on I was holding the horses. They were harnessed back to the poles and were led off. Soon the tightly tied bundles of wheat fell out of the machine. I started wondering how it knotted the string, cutting it time and time again. When I saw Father I asked him how the machine worked. He did his best to explain but as I was so young I could not understand. Soon there were rows of neat bundles around the field. The other men picked them up and stacked them in eights, in what they called 'maws', protecting the grain from ground damp.

90

The standing wheat was getting less and less until there were only a few more cuts left. You could see lots of frightened rabbits running about in it, for it had been their home whilst the crop was growing. Soon they started bolting out. Jack the terrier and Rover would go after them, almost every time catching the rabbit that had taken refuge under the stacked bundles, giving Father a great number of rabbits to gut and clean ready for the next market day. People in the town loved the young harvest rabbits – as quickly as Mother could take them from the big basket standing on the pavement the people were pushing money in her hand in order to get one.

On market day evening after the table was cleared Mother and Father talked about people and all the local gossip. Father emptied his pockets of cheques for the animals he had sold and the receipts for bills he had paid. Mother then emptied the moneybag that had been tied to her waist. Seeing that money come rolling out, and the pile of paper notes, was 'out of this world' to me. My eyes opened like barn doors as I sat there like a dog, hoping for some titbits to fall my way. All the money was counted up in paper bags and Father locked them away. Mother wrote the resulting totals into a very thick book and this too was locked away.

Nothing fell my way, so I went off to bed. As I lay in bed I began thinking about the money. In my child's mind it was lots. Where did it all come from? Why did Father take it to the bank, a place with a large polished counter? As he pushed the bag containing the money to a man sitting on the other side, he immediately emptied it out then started sorting it. Paper notes in one pile, silver and copper coins in others. Then he pulled out a large drawer from under the counter in which he put it all. I began to ask the question: "Why give that man all that money? Why didn't Father keep it all in his desk?" I said to myself that when I grew up I should keep it myself.

Next morning the conversation was concerning how the cut wheat was and how the cheeses had turned out of the cheese tubs, for they were the ones for the forthcoming cheese show. There were also concerns about the pig that had given birth to twelve little ones. In fact, they talked about all that had to be done that day and the future weeks.

That morning after finishing my jobs around the farm I went with my father to check the young heifers, which were in a field a long distance from home. When we passed the field of cut wheat Massey was looking over the binder, sharpening the cutting knives, oiling and doing any adjustments required for cutting the oats in the next field. The morning went quickly and it was time for lunch. And what was for lunch – rabbit pie! As we sat around the table Mother opened the oven door to bring out a big cooking pan of steaming hot rabbit pie covered with brown crusty pastry. It was a mouth-watering occasion. I always asked for a corner piece and a piece of rabbit from the middle of the back. Oh, that smell of hot rabbit pie when Mother first cut into it, served with new potatoes and peas all fresh from the garden. For afters, we had gooseberry and apple pie, again covered with lovely brown pastry and creamy custard. After eating we could hardly move. All the ingredients for the meal were produced on the farm, like most of our meals.

On Monday morning I was dressed ready for school. It was a big occasion for me, for I was going into the senior section. My teacher was a Miss Jones. I did not like her much for she had a hard unwelcoming voice. The bell sounded, and we all lined up to go into the first morning assembly after the holidays. The Vicar said prayers and gave a short talk on the countryside, saying how God had given us a good harvest and a warm sun so that it could be gathered in. My mind questioned all that he said for I knew it was my Father who had ploughed, sown seeds in the fields and seen it all grow. Next, Mr Wood welcomed us to the new school year, hoping we would all enjoy learning. Then we all went to our class-rooms, settling down in our place.

Miss Jones called our names for the register. Soon, in her hard voice, she set out a programme of work until Christmas. I felt unsettled and so did some of my friends who had left Miss Taylor's room. Later Miss Jones wrote a lot of figures in the form of sums on the large blackboard, telling us to add them up, or divide, as she indicated. She only came out at the end of the time she set for us to do the sums, coming around to see if we had done them correctly. If not, all she said was, "Wrong... do it again." She never explained why, or tried to explain why.

That evening I told my mother how I disliked Miss Jones and that I wasn't going to school again. Her reply was, "You are, my boy – less of that talk. You must learn to live with people you don't like. It'll be like that all your life and you have to learn how to deal with it."

Days and weeks went by, school and work on the farm fol-lowing the same old pattern. The days became wetter and colder and Massey ploughed in the fields where the corn had been. The sheep were dipped. I remember seeing the police-man standing watching it being done correctly. One day as I went home, walking through the sheep, I noticed they had all been sheared. I looked in the barn and saw all the wool rolled up in bundles ready for the wool merchants to buy.

One Saturday morning the last of the corn in the fields was ready to be brought in to the Dutch barns. That meant I had to drive the horse, taking empty drays to the field and bring back ones laden with corn. The grain was all stored in the barn, the next job with it in the future was threshing, but in the meantime the stacks became the home for rats feeding on the grain.

On Monday I was back at school for another week. As we left school in the afternoon my friend, Sam Rogers and I ran up to Tudor's bakehouse. If we were lucky Mr Tudor, for two pence, would give us two or three of the early baking fancies. Some would be mis-shaped. We did not mind. While eating we wandered along the road, up to see if Mr Turner, the blacksmith, was shoeing horses or making or repairing iron gates if he was not shoeing. He would let us work the bellows on the forge, making the fire bright and hot. Alas, he told us that the time was up and we must get on home.

One afternoon, I went home across the field where the cows were grazing. I saw one lying down on her side unable to breathe, with the tongue hanging from her mouth. She was blown up like a balloon. Realising that she was unwell I ran home as fast as I could. The first person I saw was Mother. On hearing my story she called Father who ran into the kitchen to get a surgical instrument which always hung behind the door. Off across the field he ran, with me following. He examined the cow. Next he told me to stand back, immediately plunging the instrument into the cow's side. Out came a rushing of air and liquid. Oh, what a horrible smell, which I remembered for weeks! Soon Father was raising the cow's head, pushing the tongue back into her mouth. In the meantime, the blown-up condition had gone. Soon the cow was up on her feet although she was a little wobbly. Father left, telling me to stay with the animal and if she went down again to run and tell him. All was well.

A few evenings later, when I was sitting on my stool and Father was in his chair by the fire, I asked him, "Why did that cow blow up? And how did you know where to push that pointed needle-sharp tube into her side?"

He replied in his way saying that in the morning the cows had been up in the field of new clover and she had eaten too much, or we had left them in the field too long. A gas formed in the stomach if they ate too much.

"Do horses do that, too?" I asked.

"No son, for their stomachs are different. The cow has two stomachs; one where all the food goes into first while it is grazing, then when that is full the cow lies down, then bit by bit she brings back into her mouth all the grazed material and chews it all again. Then she swallows down into a small section where it is digested into her body. It is known as 'chewing the cud' but if the gas gets too high the cow cannot deal with it, giving her what we would call a 'tummy ache', for she does not pass wind out of her stomach through the mouth or bowel like you or me, and the horse. In other words using the common words, the cow does not belch or fart. That is why the cow blows up. Oh, a young lad like you asking such questions! You'll have to be a vet when you grow up."

On another occasion I went walking in the fields with him after seeing calves being born. I asked, "How do the calves get in the cow's tummy and why does the bull get on the cow's back?"

"Because she wants him to."

"What does he do?"

"He posts a seed in the cow's letter box from which the calf grows."

"Father, why do you always look at cow-pats and sheep droppings?"

"That tells me whether their bowels are in good order and the animals are healthy."

Although Father was strict with us he always in his way explained country life and its ways to us.

As I was leaving for school one morning, Father was in conversation with a gentleman from the other end of the village who very rarely came. When I got home that afternoon mother told me that Mr Ickes, a farmer some four miles away, had foot and mouth disease in his cows. She explained how quickly it spread from farm to farm and animals sick with it had to be slaughtered and their carcasses burnt. During tea Father spoke about it to everyone, telling us he had tipped a cartload of sand in the cow yard and that he had put gallons of disinfectant on it so we and the animals could walk through it. He went on, asking if we had seen any woodpigeons' nests, for it is woodpigeons that carry the disease from farm to farm. They graze on the clover and kale heads just like cattle, then sit in the trees dropping their mess on the ground below just where the sheep and cattle wander. Father always declared war on pigeons, shooting them at every opportunity.

I asked, "Why put sand down, Father?"

"It is like this. The disease starts in the animals' feet, then they lick their feet and it spreads into the mouth. If you put down a water disinfectant it runs off their feet but disinfected sand stays on their feet much longer. Also, the animals don't like licking the sand."

The foot and mouth spread to more farms but our farm did not get infected. I often wonder if Father was right about how the disease was spread.

In the next day or two Father would be taking the cheese to Nantwich ready for the forthcoming show. Mother had prepared the butter into pound pats which had a moulded design on top of a cow. The cheese with its snow-white calico side, and the butter with the mould of the cow, looked so wonderful.

I wished I could go to the show with Father and Muriel but school had to be attended. The following days were very much the same yet things were changing. The mornings were getting colder, the cuddly little lambs had grown as big as their mothers. Some had been sold fat to the butchers to be killed for lamb chops. The little fluffy chicks had grown into cockerels and hens. Also, the little dirty brown black-birds with their speckled breasts were changing to black feathers and their beaks were turning yellow.

All around there were leaves falling from trees. Around the farm the cow houses were being whitewashed and pre-pared for the cows to stay in during the winter months. Geese and turkeys had grown fat for Christmas. In the cul-tivated fields you saw potatoes piled up then covered with straw and soil. The turnips were treated the same. These long piles were called 'hogs'. It was a way of storing them for winter food. With all this going on around me, as I walked to school, I realised my ways were changing. What people said and the answers they gave to my questions had an impor-tance to me. By now I was even beginning to understand Miss Jones, for she very often gave talks on the countryside and how we all needed each other. People, rich or poor, are all part of our lives.

In my child's mind I found it difficult to come to terms with the fact that thirty to forty young children should stand around a war memorial on a cold wet November day with the vicar saying prayers and words. We were too cold to hear. I began in my mind to question, "Would those men who were killed in a far-off land have had their children stand-ing in the wet and cold for something they did?" I did not really understand for it had happened some four years before most of us were born. That evening I spoke to Mother. She was concerned about us standing there so cold, "But you see son, that is a very small experience to what those poor men suffered on the battlefield and that is our way of saying 'thank you'. One day when you are older you'll understand what I am trying to say – perhaps when Jack Whittingham comes. You should talk to him, for he was there."

When I came home next day Muriel met me in the yard, so excited. "Victor, we have won the silver cup for the best cheese in the show!" The postman had delivered a letter informing Father of the winners of the cheese and butter classes, stating he had won the Silver Challenge Cup for the best Cheshire farmhouse cheese in England. We had also won the silver tier cakestand for our butter. The letter asked Father and Mother to attend the presentation of the trophies.

Afterwards both the cup and the cakestand stood on the big sideboard in our dining room.

CHAPTER ELEVEN

Life changes

For days now I had noticed Rover did not run about as much but slept in the hay. I asked Muriel why and she replied, "He's getting older."

At school, with Christmas coming the senior children had to put on entertainment for the parents for a party evening. Miss Jones' class was to provide the songs and a play for the evening. She chose children for different roles. I was picked for the chorus because I had a stammer when I became nervous. Also I had no singing voice. So I kept on with the lessons, not minding for now for I liked sums, drawing and writing. One day I asked the teacher why she did not put our mistakes right for us. The reply was, "You are growing up now, if I did that you would not develop your mind through thinking things out for yourself, but always rely on other people to do it for you in life."

During tea in the evenings it was a change not to talk about cows and the work of the day but the winning of the cup and the selling of the cheeses at the next cheese fair, which would be the first day of my holiday. Father hoped to get a good price from the factors.

"Father, what are factors?" I asked.

"They are the men who buy lots of cheeses then sell them to smaller shopkeepers in ones and twos," he replied.

After the school party evening the holiday started. The day arrived for the cheese fair in Market Drayton. I went with Father who was shown a place for him to place his cheeses, arranging the winning cheese at the front; stacked on the top of another was the winning cheese with the Silver Cup on top. The men came looking with their cheese probes, sampling for the taste and so on. In the afternoon the sale began. Father's cheese came first. After a short round of applause for his win, the bidding started – only reaching four pence per pound. Father was so angry that he took the cheeses back home. At tea that night he was still mad, saying that it was not worth making cheese.

Thumping the table, he declared: "I'll sell the milk to the Cadbury's dairy, that's what I'll do – for it is not worth the hard work."

The days went on with the same routines, doing jobs and feeding animals. Father had calmed down. There were signs of snow, for the mornings were very cold and frosty and the cows stayed in during the nights and part of the day, just as the year before. The geese, turkeys and fat cockerels had all been plucked and sold.

Christmas Day was just the same, the ever-familiar shirts and gloves for presents. But this Christmas I did get a clockwork Hornby train too, which gave me lots of pleasure. Sometimes, if my brother Cyril was near, he would put something on the track and the engine would become derailed. Mother got cross with him, telling him to go and do his homework or get ready for school. For now he had left the village school to attend a private college as a day boarder, which meant a daily cycle ride of ten miles.

I too had to get prepared for school. The same old routine – the only difference would be snowballing if the snow came – otherwise the year would reveal the same seasons as the years before; new leaves on the tree, lambs being born, the ploughing of the land and sowing seeds, raising new crops.

Now I was really getting used to Miss Jones and her ways.

What I liked best of all were the talks she gave on African countries including the thick forests of the jungle and how people lived. She explained how they built their houses of tree branches and palm leaves, high off the ground on posts. The floors did not have carpet like we have but large palm leaves cut from the jungle. The reason for building high off the ground was to protect them while they were sleeping from poisonous ground insects and snakes. Also living near these dense forests was a race of people called pygmies. Many times after listening to her I often wondered, "Will I go and visit them when I grow up?" Only time would tell.

When I went home that afternoon I noticed father had brought the heifers to a field near the house for they would soon be having their first baby calves. That night after tea he told me not to go near one if she had her baby for they are very protective of their first-born.

"Heifers don't close their eyes when they charge you, which helps them to follow your every move, whereas the bull closes his eyes when he charges, enabling you to step aside," he explained. "Don't go trying it out!"

One day about twenty ten-gallon milk churns were delivered, for in a few days' time the milk was to be collected for the Cadbury's processing factory. Then the remaining cheeses were to be sold to small shops.

The cheese-making equipment was put in the barn to be stored. Oh, how quiet it was in the morning with no one rushing about.

Harold, being a member of the Young Farmers' group, was going to the farm of a local farmer, who was well respected for his herd, for the evening judging of cattle. So I went with him. When we got there we were told the examiners had selected twelve cows for judging. Each young person was given a sheet of paper with the numbers of the cows written on it for them to make their own judgements.

When the judging was over, a gentleman who was giving his reactions to their skills and knowledge asked my brother, "Harold, why did you put the oldest cow first?"

His answer was, "Well, sir, I thought it must be healthy and a good milker for if not, Mr Ward would have sold it by now."

Everyone smiled. Yes, it was good thinking.

A week or two on, when I arrived home, the thrashing box was standing by the stack of oats. The steam engine was a short distance away so that a red hot spark could not fall out of the firebox and set the stacks alight. It was like a sleeping giant. Oh, how I wished I did not have to go to school next day! I thought, "Never mind, I'll run home fast tomorrow." Alas when I got home the granary storage bins were full of thrashed oats and bags of wheat for milling. The engine and all the equipment had left after doing what Father had wanted.

During tea that evening we talked about Rover being so tired and lying about a lot.

"It's his age," someone remarked.

Since the cows were in more at weekends, there was more food required. Bert would put the drive belts onto the mill and pulping machine and start the petrol engine, then all the belts moved on all the equipment. I had the job of putting the turnips into the pulper with a fork. At the other end they came out like chips, the mill grinding oats followed by some wheat flour for bread making. I cannot describe the noise. Also, we had to dodge the drive belts as we walked about.

The thrashing had provided a barn full of clean straw for the animals to lie on. Weeks went by. We got used to not having cheese to make. In fact, Father liked having a chat to the lorry driver when he collected the churns of milk each day, for he told Father of some local gossip which in turn charged the conversation at meal times.

The days at school were the same. The farm animals were fed, cleaned out and the eggs collected from the hens in the same bucketfuls, and the pigs squealed for their food.

Bert came in for breakfast one morning and had asked if anyone had seen Rover for he had not gone with him with the cows to the field. Father said, "He's probably sleeping in the hay – I'll go and have a look when I've finished my breakfast."

In a little while Father went out, only to return to the kitchen, reaching for his small gun, saying, "He's been caught in a rat trap, cutting his paws off."

I got up to go with him but Mother pulled me back. Soon we heard a shot ring out.

All Mother said was, "Poor Rover".

When he came back in, Father said one of the boys had set the trap in a rat run; leaning over it was a board to protect it from other cats and dogs. In the night the wind had blown the board away. Rover must have been looking around and being an old dog had lost too much blood – so to save him from suffering more Father thought it best to shoot him.

Later that morning I saw Bert digging a hole in the ground by an apple tree in the orchard. Beside it was a sack with Rover's body in it. That hole was to be his grave.

In the late afternoon I went up to the orchard to the mound of newly-laid turf – the outward signs of Rover's grave. While I was standing there, unnoticed by me, my father came up behind me. Putting his arm across my shoulder, he said, "Come on, son."

As we turned, me wiping a tear from my cheek with my coat sleeve, he said, "That's it, son, the end of Rover."

This is also the end of this part of my life story.

*

If you enjoyed this book you may also like these:

MEMORIES OF A CHESHIRE CHILDHOOD Lenna Bickerton (ISBN 1 901253 00 7)

Lenna describes life in Northwich around the First World War through the sharp senses of a child. Her memories are vivid: duck eggs for breakfast, dancing to Grandad's gramophone, a near tragedy at a watermill, her school-days, the sights and sounds of the old town, the smells of wild flowers, busy boat traffic on the canal — and the menacing "Ginny Greenteeth." The book also includes Lenna's obituary. £4.99

THE WAY WE WERE
Omnibus edition incorporating Over My Shoulder & Another's War
Les Cooper (ISBN 1 901253 07 4)

This is an omnibus edition of Les Cooper's Crewe memories "Over My Shoulder" and "Another's War", published separately in 1996 by Crewe & Nantwich Borough Council when the author was mayor, and now reprinted by popular demand. The first work describes his childhood in the railway town during the Depression and the second his war experiences as an apprentice in a reserved occupation at the LMS Railway Works. £7.99

NELLIE'S STORY
A Life of Service
Elizabeth Ellen Osborne (ISBN 1 901253 15 5)

Elizabeth Ellen Osborne was born at Shipbrook, near Northwich, Cheshire, in 1914. Her father was an agricultural worker and the family lived in a tied cottage. When she left school at 14 she went into service for the local 'toffs'. Following her marriage she was a nurse, a 'dinner lady' and a much-loved foster mother. As a Royal British Legion welfare officer she rode round Mid-Cheshire on a 90cc motorcycle until she was 80 years old. Nellie has a phenomenal memory and her recollections of her early life paint a vivid picture of times which have gone for ever. £5.99

DIESEL TAFF
From 'The Barracks' to Tripoli
Austin Hughes (ISBN 1 901253 14 7)

Austin Hughes was born in February 1922 at 'The Barracks', a group of flea-ridden cottages deep in rural North Wales. His book tells how he grew up innocent of the world outside. From childhood he had loved heavy machinery and he learned to drive trucks and bulldozers. Then in 1940 he was called up to join the Royal Engineers. This was to be an experience which changed the young Welshman's life and earned him his nick-name 'Diesel Taff'. By the end of the war, he'd driven thousands of miles across deserts and mountains, trans-porting heavy plant, building roads and air strips, clearing avalanches and ferrying refugees. £8.99

Léonie Press, 13 Vale Road, Hartford, Northwich, Cheshire CW8 1Pl; tel 01606 75660; fax 01606 77609; e-mail sales@leoniepress.com, website www..leoniepress.com